Mastering the
Essay

EXERCISE WORKBOOK
AP* European History Edition

by Tony Maccarella

SHERPALEARNING
GUIDING YOU TO EVEN GREATER HEIGHTS

Publisher/Editor: David Nazarian

Copy-Editor/Permissions: Christine DeFranco

Cartographer: Sal Esposito

Cover Image: Il Duomo of Florence, © shutterstock.com/Luca Villanova

Cover Design: Ivan Reynoso & David Nazarian

* AP is a registered trademark of the College Board, which was not involved in the production of, and does not endorse, this product.

ISBN 978-0-9905471-4-3

Printed in the United States of America.

10 9 8 7 6 5 4 3 2 1

Table of Contents

Also by Tony Maccarella

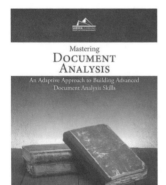

Mastering Document Analysis

An Adaptive Approach to Building Advanced Document Analysis Skills

Everything you need to master the analysis of primary and secondary source documents, *Mastering Document Analysis* is based around the same 3-step document analysis process used in *Mastering the Essay*, providing complete coverage of the skills needed to earn a top score on the AP* European History exam.

Exercises for **Ancient World History**, **Modern World History**, and **U.S. History**—available in print or digital!

[ISBN: 978-0-9905471-7-4]

How to Use this Book

Guided Practice

Each set of exercises in Part 1 of this Exercise Workbook is connected to a Guided Practice activity in the Instructional Handbook. As such, each Guided Practice can serve as a model for the exercises found in this workbook. Be sure to study each Guided Practice activity before beginning the corresponding set of exercises.

Chronological Periods

Because most European history teachers deliver their courses chronologically, each set of exercises in Part 1 of this workbook contains skills-based items organized into ascending chronological eras. This organization will help you to apply the information you are learning in school to each of the writing-skills exercises.

Updated Content and Additional Resources

As changes are made to the AP European History curriculum, we will continually update the components of *Mastering the Essay* to align with those changes.

Also, we will continue to develop new resources and activities to compliment or extend the activities found in *Mastering the Essay*.

All updates and new resources will be available to view or download through the *Mastering the Essay* page on the Sherpa Learning website. You'll also find a registration form so that we can notify you of new and updated materials.

www.sherpalearning.com/mte

Correlation Charts

A set of correlation charts is available on the Sherpa Learning website to help you target exercises by the **Historical Thinking Skills, Thematic Learning Objectives**, and **Key Concepts** laid out by the College Board® in the newly redesigned course framework for AP European History.

Historical Thinking Skill	Part 1: Practice Exercises		Part 2: Practice Tests
	The 6 Steps	The Other Question Types	
Analyzing Evidence: Content and Sourcing	Step 2 (LEQ): 1, 4, 7 Step 2 (DBQ): 1-8 Step 3: 1, 4-6 Step 4: 5, 8 Step 5B: 1-8	MC: 1, 2, 5, 6, 7 SAQ: 2, 6, 14	Test 1: 2, 3 Test 2: 2 Test 3: 2, 3
Interpretation	Step 3: 2, 3, 7 Step 5A: 1, 2, 6, 8 Step 5C: 3	SAQ: 1, 3, 4, 12	Test 1: 1 Test 2: 1 Test 3: 1
Comparison	Step 2 (LEQ): 2, 3 Step 5A: 3-5, 7	MC: 3-5 SAQ: 2, 7	Test 3: 3

Use the charts to identify all of the exercise and test questions that deal with a specific skill or concept.

By providing the correlation charts on the website, we can continually update the charts to immediately and seamlessly reflect any revisions made to the AP Euro curriculum.

To access the charts and other valuable resources, simply go to

www.sherpalearning.com/mte

Or just scan this to go directly to the site!

Part 1
Practice Exercises

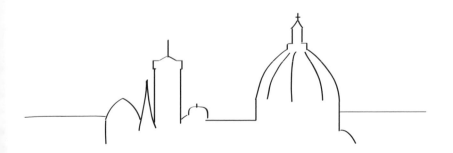

Brainstorming and Organizing Evidence

For each of the following exercises, write down as many bits of specific evidence that you think might be relevant to the terms of the question. Do not try to answer the question in your mind yet—just brainstorm terms to generate a "picture" of your knowledge of the topic.

Once the evidence is in front of you, begin to group these bits into categories that could be applied to the tasks and terms of your question. Ask yourself these questions: *How are these terms connected to each other? How might this evidence help to illustrate those connections?* The questions you pose will suggest categories—themes, concepts, and characteristics—that help to demonstrate your understanding of the terms. Ultimately, the categories you create should help to explain HOW and/or WHY your evidence addresses the tasks and terms of the question.

Directions: Read the question and identify the tasks and terms. Then, brainstorm and organize the evidence you can remember into categories that help illustrate the connections among the tasks and terms.

1. ORIGINS OF CHRISTIAN HUMANISM

Exercise Question: Assess the extent to which Christian Humanism traced its roots to Italian Humanists.

2. THE ROMAN CATHOLIC CHURCH AND ASTRONOMY

Exercise Question: Analyze the impact of Roman Catholic doctrine on the study of astronomy in the 16th and 17th centuries.

3. ENLIGHTENMENT OPTIMISM

Exercise Question: To what extent were the ideas of the Enlightenment expressions of optimism about humanity?

4. CONGRESS OF VIENNA

Exercise Question: Analyze the ways in which the Congress of Vienna used conservative political theory to create stability in post-Napoleonic Europe.

5. UNIFICATION OF ITALY AND GERMANY

Exercise Question: Compare and contrast the influence of nationalism on Italian and German unification.

6. INTERWAR ART

Exercise Question: *To what extent was Interwar Art unique from art of pre-World War I?*

7. WWII CONFERENCES AND COLD WAR POLICY

Exercise Question: *Analyze the impact of WWII Allied conferences on subsequent Cold War policy.*

8. ANTI-SOVIET UPRISINGS IN EASTERN EUROPE

Exercise Question: *Discuss the reasons for the successes and failures of anti-Soviet uprisings in Eastern Europe 1950–1989.*

2

Using the 3-Step Process to Analyze Documents for the DBQ

Directions: Identify the tasks and terms in each of the following questions, and then use the 3-Step Process to determine how each document might address those tasks and terms. Write your notes in the margins. As you analyze the documents, make a list of other specific evidence that comes to mind.

1. FRENCH WARS OF RELIGION

Exercise Question: Analyze the extent to which politics were at the heart of the French Wars of Religion 1562–1598.

Document A

SOURCE: Jeanne d'Albret, Queen of Navarre, letter to her son, Henry, February 21, 1572

In view of Margaret's judgment and the credit she enjoys with the queen her mother and the king and her brothers, if she embrace "the religion," I can say that we are the most happy people in the world, and not only our house but all the kingdom of France will share in this happiness. ... If she remain obstinate in her religion, being devoted to it, as she is said to be, it cannot be but that this marriage will prove the ruin, first, of our friends and our lands, and such a support to the papists that, with the goodwill the queen mother bears us, we shall be ruined with the churches of France.

Document B

> **SOURCE: Charles IX, King of France, letter to Jeanne d'Albret about his sister, May 1572**
>
> My dear aunt, I honor you more than the Pope, and I love my sister more than I fear him. I am not indeed a Huguenot, but neither am I a blockhead; and if the Pope play the fool too much, I will myself take Margot [Margaret of Valois] by the hand and give her away in marriage...

Document C

> **SOURCE: Salviati, Papal Nuncio, dispatch to the Cardinal Secretary of State, September 22, 1572**
>
> As to all the statements that will be made respecting the firing upon the admiral and his death, different from that which I have written to you, you will in time find out how true they are. Madame the regent, having come to be at variance with him (the admiral) and having decided upon this step a few days before, caused him to be fired upon. This was without the knowledge of the king, but with the participation of the Duke of Anjou, the Duchess of Nemours, and her son, the Duke of Guise. If the admiral had died at once, no others would have been slain. But, inasmuch as he survived, and they apprehended that some great calamity might happen should he draw closer to the king, they resolved to throw aside shame, and to have him killed together with the rest. And this was put into execution that very night.

Document D

SOURCE: **Henry of Valois, Duke of Anjou, in conversation with his physician, 1574**

Both of us were easily persuaded, and became, as it were, certain that it was the admiral who had impressed some evil and sinister opinion of us upon the king. We resolved from that moment to rid ourselves of him.... As soon as we had entered the room in which the king my brother was, my mother began to represent to him that the party of the Huguenots was arming against him on account of the wounding of the admiral....
All France would be seen armed by two great parties, over which he would have no command, and from which he could exact just as little obedience. But, to ward off so great a danger, the admiral, the head and author of all the civil wars, alone need be put to death. The designs and enterprises of the Huguenots would perish with him; and the Catholics, satisfied with the sacrifice of two or three men, would remain obedient to him (the king).

Document E

SOURCE: **Ogier Ghiselin de Busbecq, Holy Roman Emperor's ambassador to France, letter, 1575**

Ever since the commencement of the civil wars which are distracting the country, there has been a terrible change for the worse. So complete is the alteration, that those who knew France before would not recognise her again. Everywhere are to be seen shattered buildings, fallen churches, and towns in ruins; while the traveller gazes horror-stricken on spots which have but lately been the scenes of murderous deeds and inhuman cruelties. ... Besides the two parties into which Frenchmen are divided by their religious differences, there are also feuds and quarrels which affect every grade of society. ... The feuds which separate the leading families of France are more bitter than those described in ancient tragedy; this is the state of feeling which exists between the Houses of Guise, Vendôme and Bourbon, not to mention that of Montmorency, which, through its alliances and connections, has a considerable party of its own.

Document F

SOURCE: The Edict of Nantes, 1598

The realm was so torn by innumerable factions and sects that the most legitimate of all the parties was fewest in numbers. God has given us strength to stand out against this storm; ....

We have, by this perpetual and irrevocable edict, established and proclaimed and do establish and proclaim:

First, that the recollection of everything done by one party or the other between March, 1585, and our accession to the crown, and during all the preceding period of troubles, remain obliterated and forgotten, as if no such things had ever happened.

We ordain that the Catholic Apostolic and Roman religion shall be restored and reestablished in all places and localities of this our kingdom . . . in order that it may be peaceably and freely exercised, ...

And in order to leave no occasion for troubles or differences between our subjects, we have permitted, and herewith permit, those of the said religion called Reformed [Huguenots] to live and abide in all cities and places of this our kingdom . . . without being annoyed, molested, or compelled to do anything in the matter of religion contrary to their consciences....

Document G

SOURCE: **St. Bartholomew's Day Massacre by François Dubois, born 1529 in Picardy, date of painting unknown**

2. 17ᵀᴴ-CENTURY SWEDISH EMPIRE

Exercise Question: *Analyze the ways in which the monarchy impacted the success of the empire of Sweden in the 17ᵗʰ and early 18ᵗʰ centuries.*

Document A

> **SOURCE: Charles XII, future king of Sweden, in conversation with his tutor, Andreas Norcopensis (Nordenhjelm), circa 1687 (Charles was nearly 5 years old)**
>
> Nordenhjelm: "Is it right, think you, to expose one's self to danger?"— Charles: "Yes, but not too much."—N. "When do you think, then, that one is too venturesome?"—C. "When one cares for nothing at all."—N. "Now would it not be better never to expose one's self to danger?"—C. "No, for then one would be called a hare."—N. "But, surely, it is better to be called a hare and live, than to be called a lion after one is dead?"—C. "No, it would be shameful to live and be called a hare. I would rather be dead and honoured."

Document B

> **SOURCE: Charles XI, directions for his son's (Charles XII) education, circa 1690**
>
> The tutor must impress upon his pupil, on all occasions, that although he is a King's son and the heir to a great realm, nevertheless he ought always humbly to recognise this as God's special grace and favour and be diligent in acquiring those Christian virtues and necessary dispositions which can alone make him worthy of his high birth and fit for his high calling.

Document C

> **SOURCE: Declaration of Sovereignty, 1693**
>
> [Charles XI is] an all-commanding sovereign king responsible for his actions to none on earth, but with power and authority as a Christian King to rule and govern his realm as it seemeth him best.

Document D

> **SOURCE: Count D'Avaux, French ambassador, 1698**
>
> The Senators used to enter the chamber of the late King whenever they chose, and when there would converse freely and pretty loudly; but now they cannot enter without permission and, while there, must stand in respectful silence except when they whisper a word in each others' ears.

Document E

> **SOURCE: Charles XII, announcing his intention to enter war with Saxony-Poland and Denmark-Norway, 1700**
>
> I have resolved never to begin an unrighteous war; but I have also resolved never to finish a righteous war till I have utterly crushed my enemies.

Document F

> **SOURCE: Cederhjelm, Swedish officer, December 1700**
>
> God only knows what will be the end of it all, both politics and economics are treated cavalierly enough and we jog on as best we can.

Document G

> SOURCE: **Charles XII, letter to the Swedish minister at The Hague, December 1700**
>
> It would put our glory to shame, if we were to lend ourselves to the slightest treaty or accommodation with one [Augustus of Saxony] who has so vilely prostituted his honour.

3. THE DISAPPEARANCE OF POLAND

Exercise Question: *Analyze the forces inside and outside of Poland that may have contributed to the partitioning of the nation 1772–1795.*

Document A

> SOURCE: **Jerzy Niemirycz, in a speech for the ratification of the union of Hadiach, 1659**
>
> The value of the Polish Kingdom, which cannot be compared with anything, is the liberty. It is this liberty that drew us to this society. We are born and educated in this liberty, and now join to this society as free men.

Document B

SOURCE: **Sir Charles Hanbury Williams, British envoy to Saxony and Poland, a letter to Henry Fox, December 24, 1752**

I am, upon reflection, persuaded that a King of England at present has not too much Power, and that the wings of the prerogative are sufficiently clipped: a journey into Poland will convince anyone that nothing is more noxious to Society than Liberty that is degenerated into Licentiousness and where under the name of Freedom, there are more miserable slaves than in any country in the world.

Document C

SOURCE: **Soltyck, Senator of the Sejm, letter to Staeckelberg about his resignation, 1773**

I would rather sit in a dungeon and cut off my hand than sign the sentence passed on my fatherland. … a Pole who permits the partition of his country would be sinning against God. And we senators … would become perjurers.

Document D

SOURCE: **Tadeusz Rejtan, envoy to the Sejm, speech denouncing the signing of the First Partition, 1773**

On the blood of Christ, I adjure you, do not play the part of Judas; kill me, stamp on me, but do not kill the Fatherland.

Document E

SOURCE: **Count Mirabeau, writing about the First Partition of Poland, in his History of the Prussian Monarchy, 1788**

In the future, the destiny of Liberty, of Property, and of Human Life itself will be determined by the whims of despots.

Document F

SOURCE: **Karl Marx, about the Constitution of the Third of May, 1791**

With all its shortcomings, this constitution appears against the background of Russo-Prusso-Austrian barbarity as the only work of freedom which Central Europe has ever produced of its own accord. Moreover, it was created by a privileged class, the gentry. The history of the world knows no other example of such generosity by the gentry.

Document G

SOURCE: **Tadeusz Kosciuszko, Act of Insurrection of the Citizens and Inhabitants of the Palitinate of Cracow, March 24, 1794**

I, Tadeusz Kosciuszko, swear before God and to the whole Polish nation, that I shall employ the authority vested in me for the integrity of the frontiers, for gaining national self-rule and for the foundation of general liberty, and not for private benefit.

Document H

SOURCE: **Colonel William Gardner, British Minister, letter to the British Secretary of State, November 12, 1794**

It is with regret I inform your Lordship that the day of the forcing the lines of Prag was attended by the most horrid and unnecessary barbarities—Houses burnt, women massacred, infants at the breast pierced with the pikes of cosaques [Kossacks] and universal plunder, and we now know the same fate was prepared for Warsaw....

4. NAPOLEON IN EGYPT

Exercise Question: Discuss the impact of Napoleon on the culture and society of Egypt.

Document A

> **SOURCE: al-Jabarti, Egyptian historian and eyewitness to French occupation, speaking of the early 18th century, circa 1798**
>
> Egypt was glowing with beauty during that time [before Napoleon] … the poor had enough to eat, high and low alike lived comfortably.

Document B

> **SOURCE: Napoleon Bonaparte, proclamation to the people of Egypt, 1798**
>
> We, too, are true Mussulmans [Muslims]. Is it not we who have destroyed the Pope that said war must be made on the Mussulmans? Is it not we who have destroyed the Knights of Malta because those insensate chevaliers believed God wanted them to make war on the Mussulmans? Thrice happy they who are on our side! They shall prosper in their fortune and in their place. Happy those who are neutral! They shall have time to understand us, and shall array themselves with us. But woe, thrice woe, to those who shall take up arms for the Mamelukes and fight against us! There shall be no hope left for them; they shall perish.

Document C

> SOURCE: **Napoleon Bonaparte, proclamation to the people of Egypt, 1798**
>
> What wisdom, what talents, what virtues distinguish the Marmelukes, so that they have exclusive possession of everything that makes life sweet and enjoyable? Is there a fine piece of land? It belongs to the Marmelukes. Is there a beautiful slave girl, a fine horse, a handsome house? Those things too belong to the Marmelukes. If Egypt is their farm, let them show us the lease that God gave them on it!

Document D

> SOURCE: **Louis Antoine Fauvelet de Bourrienne, writing of Napoleon's order to execute Marmeluke rebels in 1798, in his memoirs, circa 1830**
>
> The sacks were opened in the principal square, and the heads rolled out before the assembled populace. I cannot describe the horror I experienced: but at the same time, I must confess that it had the effect for a considerable time of securing tranquility.

Document E

> SOURCE: **Louis Antoine Fauvelet de Bourrienne, Napoleon's secretary, in his memoirs, circa 1830**
>
> Shortly before our departure I asked Bonaparte how long he intended to remain in Egypt. He replied, "A few months, or six years: all depends on circumstances. I will colonize the country. I will bring them artists and artisans of every description; women, actors, etc. We are but nine-and-twenty now, and we shall then be five-and-thirty."

Document F

> **SOURCE: J.A. St. John, traveler to Egypt, in his memoirs, 1834**
>
> Both in the army and fleet, schools are established, where the soldiers and sailors are taught reading, writing, and arithmetic. The rude fellah from the wilds of Gournu, taken away from the fields at the age of thirty, is now daily seen bending over his slate. No soldier unable to read and write can be promoted to the rank of corporal.

Document G

> **SOURCE: Chancellor Pasquier, former member of the Parlement of Paris, commenting in his memoirs about Napoleon's reports from Egypt, date unknown**
>
> What had especially struck people in these bulletins was a certain declaration in favour of the Mohammedan creed, the effect of which, though it might be somewhat great in Egypt, had in France only called forth ridicule.

5. THE MIDDLE CLASS IN THE 19TH CENTURY

Exercise Question: *To what extent did the middle class participate in the revolutions of the 19th century?*

Document A

SOURCE: **Matthew Arnold, private secretary, in a letter to his sister, March 10, 1848**

What agitates me is this, if the new state of things succeeds in France, social changes are inevitable here and elsewhere, for no one looks on seeing his neighbour mending without asking himself if he cannot mend in the same way; but, without waiting for the result, the spectacle of France is likely to breed great agitation here, and such is the state of our masses that their movements now can only be brutal plundering and destroying. ... You must by this time begin to see what people mean by placing France politically in the van of Europe; it is the intelligence of their idea-moved masses which makes them, politically, as far superior to the insensible masses of England as to the Russian serfs.....

Document B

SOURCE: **M. Crémieux, French Minister of Justice, 1848**

In 1830, we were too hasty, and now, in 1848, we are obliged to make a fresh beginning. Let us not now be hasty; let us proceed in a more orderly, legal, and decisive manner. The provisional government that you will appoint will not only be charged with the maintenance of order, but with the introduction of measures which may protect every class of the population; in fact, of what was promised in 1830, and has not been performed.

Document C

SOURCE: Alphonse de Lamartine, French writer and politician, speech to Provisional Government of France, 1848

At great crises society stands in need of great powers. … The undefined reform which is at this day achieving its victory in the streets will not be able to assume a definite form without instantly throwing into an aggressive attitude all those classes of the people who will be excluded from the possession of power.

Document D

SOURCE: Louis Kossuth, Governor, "Abdication of the Provisional Government" of Hungary, August 11, 1849

After the defeats which have lately befallen the nation, all hope is at an end of our being able any longer to continue with success the combat in self-defence against the allied powers of Russia and Austria.

Under such circumstances, the preservation of the national existence, and the guarantee for its future, are now solely to be expected from the leader at the head of the army; … I accordingly inform the nation that, moved by that pure patriotic feeling which has led me to consecrate all my efforts, … I hereby resign and transfer the supreme civil and military power to General Arthur Gorgei, until the nation in virtue of its right shall enact otherwise.…

LOUIS KOSSUTH, Governor.

Document E

SOURCE: **Nassau William Senior, Professor of Political Economy, from a journal entry about a conversation with an Italian author, December 22, 1850**

'Do you think,' I asked, ' that the present state of things can continue?' 'No,' he answered;' it is too violent: no one in any class of society is safe. A mere denunciation to the police may occasion his arrest, and when once imprisoned he may be forgotten. ... 'But who,' I said, 'are to supply the explosive force? Not the army, for they seem devoted to the King; not the populace, for they are too degraded to care about politics; not the aristocracy, for they have not the vigour which leads men to incur great risks; and as to the middling classes, they do not seem to be sufficiently numerous.' 'What you say,' he answered, ' about the army, the mob, and the aristocracy is true; but the middle class are increasing in number, they possess almost all the intellect and education of the country, and they are unanimous. Unhappily they attempted, in 1848, to carry on together two incompatible operations—to recast all our institutions, and to make war with Austria.'

Document F

SOURCE: **Samuel Laing, author and traveler, from Observations on the Social and Political State of the European People in 1848 and 1849, published 1850**

It is a very shortsighted view of this great social movement of 1848, among the 40,000,000 of people, to attribute it to secret associations of students, or revolutionary enthusiasts, republicans, and propagandists of extravagant theories. What funds, what influence, what following, could such a class, with all their clubs and newspaper paragraphs, have in the vast, peacefully inclined, and patient German population, if the material, the enormous mass of real grievance, had not existed as a combustible prepared by the misgovernment of their rulers, and ready to catch fire from the most insignificant sparks? The Germans are a speculative people, who vindicate their intellectual freedom, and resent every attempt, open or concealed, on the right to think freely, as zealously as we would an attack upon our freedom to act in our material interests. The reason is, that their middle class is composed almost entirely of men who have no other path to distinction, social weight, and individual well-being, than through mind—through the free action of intellectual power.

Document G

SOURCE: **Nassau William Senior, Professor of Political Economy, from a journal entry, March 21, 1851**

In the provinces on the other side of the Apennines, which contain three-fourths of the population and four-fifths of the wealth of the country, the feudal system was destroyed by the French before the end of the last century or in the beginning of this. The great families were ruined, their properties and those of the rich corporations were divided, and an intelligent and numerous middle class sprang up, tolerant in religion and liberal in politics. ... It was unfortunate, therefore, that the seat of Pio Nono's reforming government was placed in Rome, where, from the want of a middle class and of political knowledge, there was, in fact, no Constitutional party. ... The real seat of constitutional liberalism is in the provinces of the Adriatic.

6. NATIONAL LEADERS OF THE GREAT WAR

Exercise Question: At the end of World War I, the victor nations assembled in Paris with the stated intention of creating a "just peace." To what extent did the delegates arrive at the Paris Peace Conference prepared to achieve this goal?

Document A

SOURCE: **Woodrow Wilson, "Fourteen Points" Speech, January 8, 1918**

It will be our wish and purpose that the processes of peace, when they are begun, shall be absolutely open and that they shall involve and permit henceforth no secret understandings of any kind. The day of conquest and aggrandizement is gone by; so is also the day of secret covenants entered into in the interest of particular governments and likely at some unlooked-for moment to upset the peace of the world.

...It is that the world be made fit and safe to live in; and particularly that it be made safe for every peace-loving nation which, like our own, wishes to live its own life, determine its own institutions, be assured of justice and fair dealing by the other peoples of the world as against force and selfish aggression. All the peoples of the world are in effect partners in this interest, and for our own part we see very clearly that unless justice be done to others it will not be done to us.

Document B

> SOURCE: **Colonel von Thaer, Excerpts of Diary Notes from October 1, 1918**
>
> For the cited reasons we could no longer allow ourselves to be beaten. Therefore, the Supreme Army Command demanded of His Majesty the Kaiser and of the Chancellor that a proposal for the bringing about of peace be made to President Wilson of America without delay, for bringing about an armistice on the basis of his 14 Points. He said he had never shied away from demanding the utmost from his troops. However, after clearly realizing that the continuation of the war was useless, he was of the opinion that an end needed to be found as quickly as possible in order not to unnecessarily sacrifice the most valiant people who were still loyal and able to fight.
>
> It had been a terrible moment for him and for the Field Marshall to have to report this to His Majesty the Kaiser and the Chancellor.

Document C

> SOURCE: **Allied Armistice Terms, November 11, 1918**
>
> One– Cessation of operations by land and in the air six hours after the signature of the armistice.
>
> Two– Immediate evacuation of invaded countries: Belgium, France, Alsace-Lorraine, Luxemburg, so ordered as to be completed within fourteen days from the signature of the armistice. German troops which have not left the above-mentioned territories within the period fixed will become prisoners of war.
>
> Three– Reparation beginning at once to be completed within fifteen days of all the inhabitants of the countries above enumerated (including hostages, persons under trial or convicted).

Document D

SOURCE: **Georges Clemenceau, Opening Address as President at the Paris Peace Conference, January 18, 1919**

I come now to the order of the day. The first question is as follows: "The responsibility of the authors of the war." The second is thus expressed: "Penalties for crimes committed during the war." ... If we wish to establish justice in the world we can do so now, for we have won victory and can impose the penalties demanded by justice. ... We shall insist on the imposition of penalties on the authors of the abominable crimes committed during the war.

Document E

SOURCE: **Count von Brockdorff-Rantzau, Leader of the German Peace Delegation, Letter to Paris Peace Conference President Georges Clemenceau on the Subject of Peace Terms, May 1919**

We came to Versailles in the expectation of receiving a peace proposal based on the agreed principles. We were firmly resolved to do everything in our power with a view of fulfilling the grave obligations which we had undertaken. We hoped for the peace of justice which had been promised to us.

We were aghast when we read in documents the demands made upon us, the victorious violence of our enemies. The more deeply we penetrate into the spirit of this treaty, the more convinced we become of the impossibility of carrying it out. The exactions of this treaty are more than the German people can bear.

Document F

SOURCE: **Georges Clemenceau, Letter of Reply to the Objections of the German Peace Delegation, May 1919**

The protest of the German Delegation shows that they utterly fail to understand the position in which Germany stands today. They seem to think that Germany has only to "make sacrifices in order to attain peace," as if this were but the end of some mere struggle for territory and power.

The Allied and Associated Powers therefore feel it necessary to begin their reply by a clear statement of the judgment passed upon the war by practically the whole of civilized mankind.

In the view of the Allied and Associated Powers the war which began on August 1, 1914, was the greatest crime against humanity and the freedom of peoples that any nation, calling itself civilized, has ever consciously committed.

…Germany's responsibility, however, is not confined to having planned and started the war. She is no less responsible for the savage and inhuman manner in which it was conducted.

…They were the first to use poisonous gas, notwithstanding the appalling suffering it entailed. They began the bombing and long distance shelling of towns for no military object, but solely for the purpose of reducing the morale of their opponents by striking at their women and children. They commenced the submarine campaign with its piratical challenge to international law, and its destruction of great numbers of innocent passengers and sailors, in mid-ocean, far from succour, at the mercy of the winds and the waves, and the yet more ruthless submarine crews.

Document G

SOURCE: **Dutch Algemeen Handelsblad Editorial on the Treaty of Versailles, June 1919**

The peace conditions imposed upon Germany are so hard, so humiliating, that even those who have the smallest expectation of a "peace of justice" are bound to be deeply disappointed.

Has Germany actually deserved such a "peace"? Everybody knows how we condemned the crimes committed against humanity by Germany. Everybody knows what we thought of the invasion of Belgium, the submarine war, the Zeppelin raids.

…This "peace" offered to Germany may differ in form from the one imposed upon conquered nations by the old Romans, but certainly not in essence. This peace is a mockery of President Wilson's principles. Trusting to these, Germany accepted peace. That confidence has been betrayed in such a manner that we regard the present happenings as a deep humiliation, not only to all governments and nations concerned in this peace offer, but to all humanity.

---

7. DECOLONIZATION

Exercise Question: *Describe and analyze the various attitudes toward decolonization 1930–1960.*

Document A

SOURCE: **Mohandas K. Gandhi, interview with the *Times of India*, March 12, 1930**

In spite of a forest of books containing rules and regulations, the only law the nation knows is the will of the British administrators, and the only public peace the nation knows is the peace of the public prison. India is one vast prison house. I repudiate this law, and regard it as my sacred duty to break the mournful monotony of compulsory peace that is choking the nation's heart for want of a free vent.

Document B

SOURCE: **"Burma: Statement of Policy by His Majesty's Government," May 1945**

The considered policy of His Majesty's Government of promoting full self-government in Burma has frequently been declared. It is and has consistently been our aim to assist her political development till she can sustain the responsibilities of complete self-government within the British Commonwealth... .

Inevitably Burma's progress towards full self-government has been interrupted and set back by, the Japanese invasion and the long interval of enemy occupation and active warfare in her territories, during which she has suffered grave damage not only in the form of material destruction but in a shattering of the foundations of her economic and social life. It is, of course, upon these foundations that a political structure rests, and until the foundations are once again firm the political institutions which were in operation before the Japanese invasion cannot be restored... .

Document C

SOURCE: **President Sukarno of Indonesia, Speech at the Opening of the Bandung Conference, April 18 1955**

All of us, I am certain, are united by more important things than those which superficially divide us. We are united, for instance, by a common detestation of colonialism in whatever form it appears. We are united by a common detestation of racialism. And we are united by a common determination to preserve and stabilise peace in the world. ...

We are often told "Colonialism is dead." Let us not be deceived or even soothed by that. I say to you, colonialism is not yet dead. How can we say it is dead, so long as vast areas of Asia and Africa are unfree.

Document D

SOURCE: **Prime Minister Nehru, speech to Bandung Conference Political Committee, 1955**

If I join any of these big groups I lose my identity. ... If all the world were to be divided up between these two big blocs what would be the result? The inevitable result would be war. Therefore every step that takes place in reducing that area in the world which may be called the unaligned area is a dangerous step and leads to war... .

Therefore, are we, the countries of Asia and Africa, devoid of any positive position except being pro-communist or anti-communist? Has it come to this, that the leaders of thought who have given religions and all kinds of things to the world have to tag on to this kind of group or that and be hangers-on of this party or the other carrying out their wishes and occasionally giving an idea? It is most degrading and humiliating to any self-respecting people or nation. It is an intolerable thought to me that the great countries of Asia and Africa should come out of bondage into freedom only to degrade themselves or humiliate themselves in this way...

Document E

SOURCE: **The "Loi-Cadre," Article 4, June 23, 1956**

The Government may ... take all measures intended to raise the standard of living in the territories under the jurisdiction of the Ministry of France Overseas, to promote economic development and social progress and to facilitate economic and financial cooperation between Metropolitan France and those territories, especially:

By generalizing and standardizing education;

By organizing and supporting the production of goods necessary to the economic equilibrium of the territories and to the needs of the franc area; ...

By taking all measures calculated to ensure a successful social program...

Document F

SOURCE: **Anwar el Sadat, address delivered at the First Afro-Asian People's Solidarity Conference, December 26, 1957**

Because our Conference is a Conference of peoples, it has been able to muster, not only the countries recognized by International Law as independent units, but also those peoples whose status is a foregone conclusion, a historical fact, and a reality endorsed by the whole of mankind, in addition to peoples who are still trodden under the heel of imperialism in one form or another. But our Conference takes the interest of these very peoples to heart. They are the diseased organs in the body of Asia and Africa: consequently they stand in dire need of the greatest of care and attention. A body cannot continue to exist with half of its structure safe and sound while the other half is diseased and decayed... .

Document G

SOURCE: United Nations, Declaration on Granting Independence to Colonial Countries and Peoples, 1960

Recognizing that the peoples of the world ardently desire the end of colonialism in all its manifestations...

Believing that the process of liberation is irresistible and irreversible and that, in order to avoid serious crises, an end must be put to colonialism and all practices of segregation and discrimination associated therewith...

Convinced that all peoples have an inalienable right to complete freedom, the exercise of their sovereignty and the integrity of their national territory,

Solemnly proclaims the necessity of bringing to a speedy and unconditional end colonialism in all its forms and manifestations;

And to this end Declares that ... Inadequacy of political, economic, social or educational preparedness should never serve as a pretext for delaying independence... .

8. EUROPEAN UNIFICATION

Exercise Question: *Explain the attitudes toward European unification, 1950–1990.*

Document A

SOURCE: **Jean Monnet, declaration to create the ECSC, May 1950**

Through the consolidation of basic production and the institution of a new High Authority, whose decisions will bind France, Germany and the other countries that join, this proposal represents the first concrete step towards a European federation, imperative for the preservation of peace.

Document B

SOURCE: **Averell Harriman, special U.S. representative to supervise European recovery, cable from Paris, 1950**

...the [Monnet] proposal may well prove most important step towards economic progress and peace of Europe since original Marshall [Plan] speech [of 5 June 1947] ... It is first indication of bold, imaginative, concrete initiative on part of European country in attacking two basic problems ... integration of European economy and conclusive alignment of Germany on side of West with minimum political and economic complications.

Document C

> **SOURCE: Treaty of Rome, March 25, 1957**
>
> His Majesty The King of the Belgians, the President of the Federal Republic of Germany, the President of the French Republic, the President of the Italian Republic, Her Royal Highness The Grand Duchess of Luxembourg, Her Majesty The Queen of the Netherlands,
>
> Determined to lay the foundations of an ever closer union among the peoples of Europe,
>
> Resolved to ensure the economic and social progress of their countries by common action to eliminate the barriers which divide Europe... .

Document D

> **SOURCE: Charles de Gaulle, French President, speech delivered at his tenth press conference, July 23, 1964**
>
> The governments of nations alone can be capable of and responsible for making policy. It is of course not forbidden to imagine that a day will come when all the peoples of our continent will become one and that then there could be a Government of Europe, but it would be ridiculous to act as if that day had come.
>
> That is why France—refusing to let Europe get bogged down, becoming bogged down herself in a guileful undertaking that would have stripped States, misled peoples and prevented the independence of our continent— took the initiative of proposing to her five partners of the Rome Treaty a beginning for the organization of their cooperation. Thus, we would begin to live in common, pending the time when habit and evolution would gradually draw the tics closer together.

Document E

> **SOURCE: Maurice Couve de Murville, French Foreign Minister, speech to the French National Assembly, April 14, 1966**
>
> That is the problem, for the United States occupies such an important— shall I say such a predominant—place in NATO that if one touches the Organization, one seems to take issue with the United States itself. It happens, for the same reason, that the foreign forces stationed in Europe, outside of Germany, are almost entirely American forces.... .
>
> It is inevitable, and beneficial to all, that Europe reassume its independence with respect to America.

Document F

> **SOURCE: Robert Marjolin, Memoirs 1911-1986: Architect of European Unity, published 1989**
>
> As for the position of General de Gaulle and the Gaullists … it can be summed up thus: today and for all time, the fundamental political reality is and will be the nation-state; the latter may, by treaty concluded with other nation-states, relinquish certain tokens of its sovereignty, but these can only be individual and specific relinquishments, carefully defined and explicitly agreed to.

Document G

> **SOURCE: Labour Euro-safeguards Campaign, 1998**
>
> Unless and until the different people of Europe feel that they are European more than they are French, German, British, etc., no European Parliament whatever its powers, could obtain legitimacy and authority for decision.

Part A—
Thesis Recognition

Directions: In order to write an excellent thesis, it helps to know what one looks like. In these exercises, you will read sample essay questions followed by several possible thesis responses. Since the new rubric awards one point for an acceptable thesis and an additional point for developing an appropriate argument through further analysis, you should rate each thesis with a 0, 1, or 2.

Before you begin, review the Long Essay Rubric Guide on page 7 of the Instructional Handbook to familiarize yourself with the thesis qualities that correspond with each score. Begin each exercise by identifying the TASKS and TERMS of the question. Next, read the thesis statements below the question, and on the line beside each thesis, provide the score that you think it deserves—0, 1, or 2.

1. CATHOLIC REFORMATION IN SPAIN

Exercise Question: Describe and compare the components of the Catholic Reformation in Spain.

Possible Thesis Statement Responses:

_____ **A.** Among the components of the Catholic Reformation in Spain were the Jesuits, who worked through education and conversion; the Inquisition, which operated through fear; and the monarchy, which used conquest and royal edict to conduct Reformation activities.

_____ **B.** In Spain, the Catholic Reformation was very different from other parts of Europe because it was supported by Ferdinand and Isabella.

_____ **C.** The Catholic Reformation in Spain had many components.

_____ **D.** The Catholic Reformation in Spain included the Inquisition, the Jesuits, and the monarchy.

_____ **E.** The Catholic Reformation was more accurately named the Counter Reformation because it was actually a "counter" to the Protestant Reformation started by Martin Luther.

_____ **F.** The components of the Catholic Reformation in Spain were very diverse.

_____ **G.** The Inquisition, the Jesuits, and the Spanish monarchy were all components of the Catholic Reformation in Spain.

2. GROWTH OF PARLIAMENTARY POWER IN ENGLAND

Exercise Question: _Discuss the reasons for the growth of Parliamentary power in England 1625–1688._

Possible Thesis Statement Responses:

_____ **A.** Charles I opposed Parliament in the English Civil War, which led to the eventual loss of his head. As Parliament's power grew, it was able to negotiate an agreement with a new king and queen, William and Mary.

_____ **B.** Heavy war debt, which led to a need for Parliament's approval of more taxes; the monarchy's refusal to negotiate with Parliament, which led to a military engagement and regicide; and the willingness of William and Mary to accept Parliament's invitation to the throne in 1688, which formalized Parliament's claims to power, combined to extend the power of Parliament in England 1625–1688.

_____ **C.** Parliament's power grew in England 1625–1688 because King Charles I, who needed money, refused to compromise with Parliament; the subsequent war, which was won by Parliament; and the eventual deal struck with William and Mary.

_____ **D.** Parliament's power grew in England 1625–1688 because of the mismanagement of the state by the Stuart monarchies, which led to a heavier tax burden, and the ability of Parliament to use the monarchy's economic problems to its own advantage.

_____ **E.** Parliament's power grew in England 1625–1688 because Oliver Cromwell led the Roundheads to victory at Marston Moor and beheaded the king. Cromwell then went on to reduce Parliament to a "Rump" of his staunchest supporters and proclaim himself Lord Protector. Despite his inability to create a hereditary claim to his position, Parliament's power still grew stronger than it had ever been before.

_____ **F.** The reasons for the growth of Parliamentary power in England 1625-1688 can be summed up as economic, political, and social.

_____ **G.** There were many reasons for the growth of Parliamentary power in England 1625–1688.

3. ENLIGHTENED DESPOTS

Exercise Question: _To what extent was the reign of Frederick the Great of Prussia more "enlightened" than that of Joseph II of Austria?_

Possible Thesis Statement Responses:

_____ **A.** Frederick the Great was ultimately more successful than Joseph II because Frederick's monarchy was more absolute.

_____ **B.** Frederick the Great's reign was more enlightened than that of Joseph II of Austria to a very great extent.

_____ **C.** Joseph II of Austria was a child of the Enlightenment while Frederick the Great was a Prussian militarist, making his reign more enlightened to a very little, if any, extent.

_____ **D.** Politically and socially, Frederick was more enlightened because he created a law code that provided for legal equality and religious freedom. Economically, he refused to release the serfs or abolish noble privileges, so Frederick the Great was not more enlightened than Joseph.

_____ **E.** There are several political, economic, and social reasons that Frederick the Great was more enlightened than Joseph II.

_____ **F.** To the extent that the Prussian Code instituted equality before the law and religious freedom, the reign of Frederick the Great was more enlightened than that of Joseph II, but to the extent that Joseph's reforms were enacted for the sake of reforming Austrian society, while Frederick acted primarily to enhance the power of the monarchy, Frederick was less enlightened than Joseph.

_____ **G.** While his Prussian Code made all Prussians equal before the law and allowed for complete freedom of religion, Frederick the Great acted primarily to enhance the power of the Prussian monarchy, not that of the people, so his reign was not as enlightened as that of Joseph II.

4. NAPOLEON AS ANTI-REVOLUTIONARY

Exercise Question: *Assess the extent to which Napoleon I was anti-revolutionary.*

Possible Thesis Statement Responses:

_____ **A.** Because Napoleon had been a Jacobin during the revolution and he never wanted to be king, he was obviously not anti-revolutionary.

_____ **B.** Napoleon I continued the spirit of the French Revolution through his law code, which made all citizens equal before the law; his education reforms, which expanded opportunities for the wealthier classes; and his economic reforms, starting with the Bank of France.

_____ **C.** Napoleon I was a very good leader because he started the Napoleonic Code, education reforms, and economic reforms.

_____ **D.** Napoleon I was anti-revolutionary to a great extent.

_____ **E.** Napoleon I was anti-revolutionary to a small extent.

_____ **F.** Napoleon I was not at all anti-revolutionary because of his Napoleonic Code, education reforms, and his economic reforms.

_____ **G.** To the extent that Napoleon I ruled with almost absolute power, he had violated the principles of popular sovereignty on which much of the revolution had been built; however, to the extent that, even as an absolutist, Napoleon often acted in the interests of the French people, and the Napoleonic Code edified many of the legal reforms begun earlier in the revolution, he was not at all anti-revolutionary.

5. INDUSTRIALIZATION AND SOCIAL CHANGE

Exercise Question: *Analyze the impact of the Industrial Revolution on the lower classes of Europe in the 19ᵗʰ century.*

Possible Thesis Statement Responses:

_____ **A.** As a result of the Industrial Revolution, lower-class families were broken down because all members of the family needed to work outside the home; lower-class children were less educated because their families needed them to work from a very young age; and lower-class women were often driven to prostitution because it paid more than factory work.

_____ **B.** Exploitation! That was the impact of the Industrial Revolution on the lower classes in Europe in the 19ᵗʰ century: wage exploitation, child exploitation, and sexual exploitation.

_____ **C.** Industrialists, like John D. Rockefeller and J.P. Morgan, benefited from the Industrial Revolution, while lower-class people suffered the underside of the "gilded age."

_____ **D.** The Industrial Revolution affected the living conditions, working conditions, and social structure of the lower classes in Europe in the 19ᵗʰ century.

_____ **E.** The Industrial Revolution created several social, economic, and political disadvantages for lower-class people in Europe in the 19ᵗʰ century.

_____ **F.** The negative side of the Industrial Revolution hit the lowest classes the hardest in nineteenth-century Europe.

_____ **G.** While the Industrial Revolution created new opportunities for urban workers, low wages and poor working conditions disadvantaged the lowest economic classes of nineteenth-century Europe.

6. CAUSES OF WORLD WAR I

Exercise Question: *To what extent was militarism a major cause of World War I?*

Possible Thesis Statement Responses:

_____ **A.** Although Germany and Britain were engaged in a naval arms race and Germany and France each adhered to strategies that promised to eliminate the other quickly, the real cause of WWI was Germany's underestimation of the Russian military. If the Kaiser had respected Russia's strength, he may not have stood by while Austria-Hungary provoked a war in the Balkans.

_____ **B.** Kaiser Wilhelm's desire to test his new navy and demonstrate German superiority on the continent, encouraged by the outcome promised by the Schlieffen Plan, proves militarism was the root cause of World War I.

_____ **C.** Like most other wars, WWI was caused by greed for more land and more resources.

_____ **D.** Militarism was a major cause of WWI to a very great extent.

_____ **E.** Since the arms race produced new weapons that the great powers wanted to try out, and strategies like the Schlieffen Plan inspired their leaders to believe that they could each win quickly, militarism was a major cause of WWI. The fact that the conflict became a "world war," however, resulted more from the diplomatic arrangements that had been forming since the 1870s.

_____ **F.** To the extent that the great powers were engaged in an arms race that resulted in new weapons on land and at sea, and France and Germany each developed plans to destroy the other on the battlefield, militarism was a major cause of World War I; however, to the extent that the arms race and war games were the result of the hubris and short-sightedness of the leaders of these nations, militarism was merely a byproduct.

_____ **G.** World War I was caused by several factors, including politics, economics, and militarism.

7. IMPORTANCE OF THE MARSHALL PLAN

Exercise Question: *Assess the importance of the Marshall Plan in Europe's postwar recovery.*

Possible Thesis Statement Responses:

_____ **A.** The Marshall Plan was very important to Europe's postwar recovery.

_____ **B.** Because Marshall Plan monies amounted to only about 5% of Western Europe's GNP and several countries had already achieved prewar production levels by 1948, the Marshall Plan was not essential to European recovery; however, the fact that Marshall Plan rules required the cooperation of European nations and helped to inspire the formation of the ECSC, which led to the EU, the Marshall Plan can be said to have maximized long-term growth in postwar Europe.

_____ **C.** Because the Marshall Plan led to the European Coal & Steel Community, which led to the European Economic Community, which eventually led to the European Union, the Marshall Plan played a major role in postwar European recovery.

_____ **D.** Although Marshall's ideas helped European recovery, it was the ideas of men like Schuman and Monnet that guided the reorganization of Europe's economies and eventually led to the Common Market and European Union, both of which made Europe economically greater than the sum of its parts.

_____ **E.** Since the Marshall Plan did nothing for Eastern Europe, it was not a major factor in postwar recovery. Instead the

Marshall Plan was a cynical attempt to impose American democracy on an unwilling, but vulnerable, Europe.

_____ **F.** The Marshall Plan helped Europe recover economically, restructure socially, and restabilize politically.

_____ **G.** By outlawing warfare, the Marshall Plan helped Europe to recover after WWI, but alas it was impossible to prevent another world war.

8. EUROPE'S COMMON CURRENCY

Exercise Question: *Discuss the arguments in favor of a common currency in Europe 1980–2000.*

Possible Thesis Statement Responses:

_____ **A.** Those in favor of adopting the Euro argued that a single currency would save each nation millions of dollars in exchange fees, that a currency used by all Europeans would be much more stable and so compete well with the almighty dollar, and that the added stability would tend to lower interest rates within Europe, thereby promoting further growth.

_____ **B.** Many people made many different arguments in favor of a common currency in Europe 1980-2000, even though there were others who argued against it.

_____ **C.** Exchange fees and the strengthening of weaker currencies against the US dollar were both arguments in favor of the Euro.

_____ **D.** National currencies like the lira in Italy had become so inflated that it took 20,000 of them just to buy a bottle of wine. The Euro would fix all this and not be so inflated.

_____ **E.** There were definitely social, political, as well as economic arguments in favor of a common currency in Europe 1980–2000.

_____ **F.** Although there were arguments in favor of a common currency in Europe 1980-2000, there were many more arguments against it. Some people argued that the rich nations would have to support the poor nations and that a common currency involved too much loss of national autonomy.

_____ **G.** Germans argued that the Euro would reduce exchange fees, while the Italians supported it because it would be more stable than their currency, and the French saw the Euro as a way to compete with the US currency.

Part B—
Analytical Thesis Development

Directions: For each of the exercises in this set, follow the model you learned to develop a thesis that answers the question. Be sure to complete each step of the prewriting process to insure that your response is well organized.

Step 1: Identify the tasks and terms
Step 2: Brainstorm specific evidence

Finally, craft your analytical thesis statement.

1. ORIGINS OF CHRISTIAN HUMANISM

Exercise Question: *Assess the extent to which Christian Humanism traced its roots to Italian Humanists.*

2. THE ROMAN CATHOLIC CHURCH AND ASTRONOMY

Exercise Question: *Analyze the impact of Roman Catholic doctrine on the study of astronomy in the 16th and 17th centuries.*

3. ENLIGHTENMENT OPTIMISM

Exercise Question: *To what extent were the ideas of the Enlightenment expressions of optimism about humanity?*

4. CONGRESS OF VIENNA

Exercise Question: *Analyze the ways in which the Congress of Vienna used conservative political theory to create stability in post-Napoleonic Europe.*

5. UNIFICATION OF ITALY AND GERMANY

Exercise Question: *Compare and contrast the influence of nationalism on Italian and German unification.*

6. INTERWAR ART

Exercise Question: *To what extent was art of the interwar period driven by reaction to World War I?*

7. WWII CONFERENCES AND COLD WAR POLICY

Exercise Question: Analyze the impact of WWII Allied conferences on subsequent Cold War policy.

8. ANTI-SOVIET UPRISINGS IN EASTERN EUROPE

Exercise Question: Discuss the reasons for the successes and failures of anti-Soviet uprisings in Eastern Europe 1950–1989.

Presenting the Argument

Directions: For this set of exercises, you will practice all the skills covered so far in this book:

Step 1: Identify the tasks and terms

Step 2: Brainstorm specific evidence

Step 3: Develop a thesis and categories of evidence, and then outline your argument

Next, use the argument laid out in the given thesis to develop an opening paragraph. Remember that your opening should explain the WHYs and/or HOWs of your categories of evidence. Use the sentences of this paragraph to clearly connect each category of evidence to your main point.

1. CATHOLIC REFORMATION IN SPAIN

Exercise Question: *Describe and analyze the components of the Catholic Reformation in Spain.*

Thesis: Among the components of the Catholic Reformation in Spain were the Jesuits, who worked through education and conversion; the Inquisition, which operated through fear; and the monarchy, which used conquest and royal edict to conduct Reformation activities.

2.   GROWTH OF PARLIAMENTARY POWER IN ENGLAND

Exercise Question: *Discuss the reasons for the growth of Parliamentary power in England 1625–1688.*

Thesis: Heavy war debt, which led to a need for Parliament's approval of more taxes; the monarchy's refusal to negotiate with Parliament, which led to a military engagement and regicide; and the willingness of William and Mary to accept Parliament's invitation to the throne in 1688, which formalized Parliament's claims to power, combined to extend the power of Parliament in England 1625-1688.

3.   ENLIGHTENED DESPOTS

Exercise Question: *To what extent was the reign of Frederick the Great of Prussia more "enlightened" than that of Joseph II of Austria?*

Thesis: To the extent that the Prussian Code instituted equality before the law and religious freedom, the reign of Frederick the Great was more enlightened than that of Joseph II, but to the extent that Joseph's reforms were enacted for the sake of reforming Austrian society, while Frederick acted primarily to enhance the power of the monarchy, Frederick was less enlightened than Joseph.

4.   NAPOLEON AS ANTI-REVOLUTIONARY

Exercise Question: *Assess the extent to which Napoleon I was anti-revolutionary.*

Thesis: To the extent that Napoleon I ruled with almost absolute power, he had violated the principles of popular sovereignty on which much of the revolution had been built; however, to the extent that, even as an absolutist, Napoleon often acted in the interests of the French people, and the Napoleonic Code edified many of the legal reforms begun earlier in the revolution, he was not at all anti-revolutionary.

5. INDUSTRIALIZATION AND SOCIAL CHANGE

Exercise Question: Analyze the impact of the Industrial Revolution on the lower classes of Europe in the 19th century.

Thesis: As a result of the Industrial Revolution, lower-class families were broken down because all members of the family needed to work outside the home; lower-class children were less educated because their families needed them to work from a very young age; and lower-class women were often driven to prostitution because it paid more than factory work.

6. CAUSES OF WORLD WAR I

Exercise Question: To what extent was militarism a major cause of World War I?

Thesis: To the extent that the great powers were engaged in an arms race that resulted in new weapons on land and at sea, and France and Germany each developed plans to destroy the other on the battlefield, militarism was a major cause of World War I; however, to the extent that the arms race and war games were the result of the hubris and short-sightedness of the leaders of these nations, militarism was merely a byproduct.

7. IMPORTANCE OF THE MARSHALL PLAN

Exercise Question: Assess the importance of the Marshall Plan in Europe's postwar recovery.

Thesis: Because Marshall Plan monies amounted to only about 5% of Western Europe's GNP and several countries had already achieved prewar production levels by 1948, the Marshall Plan was not essential to European recovery; however, the fact that Marshall Plan rules required the cooperation of European nations and helped to inspire the formation of the ECSC, which led to the EU, the Marshall Plan can be said to have maximized long-term growth in postwar Europe.

8. EUROPE'S COMMON CURRENCY

Exercise Question: Discuss the arguments in favor of a common currency in Europe 1980–2000.

Thesis: Those in favor of adopting the Euro argued that a single currency would save each nation millions of dollars in exchange fees, that a currency used by all Europeans would be much more stable and so compete well with the almighty dollar, and that the added stability would tend to lower interest rates within Europe, thereby promoting further growth.

Part A—Analyzing Evidence for the Long Essay Question (LEQ)

Directions: For this set of exercises, you will practice all the skills covered so far in this book:

Step 1: Identify the tasks and terms

Step 2: Brainstorm specific evidence

Step 3: Develop a thesis and categories of evidence, and then outline your argument

Step 4: Write an opening paragraph

Then, using your outline as a guide, write three body paragraphs, remembering that each time you introduce new evidence, you must also explicitly state why it matters to your thesis. Don't worry about writing style, transitions, or the closing—those things will be covered later in the book. Additionally, don't worry about timing and pacing. For now, it is more important to focus all of your attention on developing a written response that meets all the requirements of the AP LEQ rubric.

1. ELIZABETHAN ENGLAND

Exercise Question: To what extent was the England of Elizabeth I religiously tolerant?

2. THEORIES OF ASTRONOMY

Exercise Question: *Describe the ways in which the pursuit of astronomical theories changed the landscape in other fields of science and math. Analyze the reasons for this interaction.*

3. ROOTS OF SOCIAL CONTRACT THEORIES

Exercise Question: *Identify and analyze the events of the 17th century that influenced the social contract theories of Hobbes and Locke.*

4. FRENCH REVOLUTION AND WOMEN

Exercise Question: *Analyze the ways in which women actively participated in the French Revolution.*

5. REVOLUTIONS OF 1848

Exercise Question: *To what extent were the Revolutions of 1848 successful?*

6. IMPACT OF TECHNOLOGY 1900–1918

Exercise Question: *Identify and assess the impact of new technology on the conduct of the Great War.*

7. ECONOMIC IMPACT OF WORLD WAR II

Exercise Question: In what ways and for what reasons did WWII affect European economies after 1945?

8. EVOLUTION OF THE EUROPEAN UNION

Exercise Question: To what extent did British decisions help shape the European Union?

Part B—Analyzing Evidence for the DBQ

Directions: For this set of exercises, you will practice all the skills covered so far in this book:

Step 1: Identify the tasks and terms

Step 2: Brainstorm specific evidence

Step 3: Develop a thesis and categories of evidence, and then outline your argument

Step 4: Write an opening paragraph

Then, using your outline as a guide, write three body paragraphs, remembering that each time you introduce a new document or piece of specific evidence, you must state explicitly why it matters to your thesis. Critically analyze the source wherever you can and, for each document, develop the habit of combining a contextual citation with a sentence-ending parenthetical citation.

1. BAROQUE ART

Exercise Question: *Analyze the ways in which Baroque artists of Italy differed from their contemporaries in the Netherlands.*

Document A

SOURCE: Caravaggio, *The Supper at Emmaus*, 1601

Document B

SOURCE: **Guido Reni, Italian artist, speaking of Rubens, circa 1620**

The fellow mixes blood with his colors.

Document C

SOURCE: **Peter Paul Rubens, in his memoirs, circa 1640**

My talent is of such a kind that no commission, however great in size or varied in subject matter, ever daunted me.

Document D

SOURCE: **Rembrandt van Rijn, *The Money Changer (Parable of a Rich Man)*, 1627**

Document E

SOURCE: **John Evelyn, English traveler to Rome, 1644**

Bernini, a Florentine sculptor, architect, painter, and poet, gave a public opera . . . wherein he painted the scenes, cut the statues, invented the engines, composed the music, writ the comedy, and built the theater.

Document F

> **SOURCE: Joachim von Sandrart, art historian and painter, about Rembrandt upon his death, circa 1669**
>
> What he chiefly lacked was knowledge of Italy, and of other places which afford opportunities for the study of the antique and of the theory of art... His art suffered from his predilection for the society of the vulgar.

Document G

> **SOURCE: John Ruskin, nineteenth-century English art critic, about Rembrandt, circa 1888**
>
> Vulgarity, dullness, or impiety will always express themselves through art in brown and grays as in Rembrandt.... It is the aim of the best painters to paint the noblest things they can see by sunlight. It was the aim of Rembrandt to paint the foulest things he could see—by rushlight [primitive candle].

2. SPANISH LITERATURE

Exercise Question: *In what ways were the Spanish writers of the Golden Age influenced by the conquistadors and their legends of chivalry?*

Document A

> **SOURCE: Juan Luis Vives, Spanish humanist, *De disciplinis*, 1531**
>
> What pleasure can be derived from such unbelievable adventures? This man killed twenty enemies, all by himself; the other killed thirty. Another one, pierced by six hundred wounds and abandoned as dead, the next day arises fresh and healthy, puts up a tremendous fight against two enormous giants, and gets out of it with so much silver, gold, silk, and jewelry that not even a galley could transport it.

Document B

SOURCE: **Juan Luis Vives, Spanish humanist,** *De disciplinis*, **1531**

Women should study for their own sake, or, in the best case, for the education of their children as long as they are very little. It is not proper for a woman to be in charge of schools, to socialize with strange men, to speak in public.... . The honest woman stays at home, unknown to others. In public meetings she should keep her eyes down, be silent and modest, seen but not heard.

Document C

SOURCE: **Luis de Góngora, Spanish poet, "Ode to the Armada," pre-1588**

O Island! Once so Catholic, so strong,

Fortress of faith, now Heresy's foul shrine,

...Of Arthurs, Edwards, Henries! Where are they?

...Condemned, thou guilty blame

Of her who rules thee now.

O hateful Queen so hard of heart and brow,

Wanton by turns, and cruel, fierce, and lewd.... .

Document D

SOURCE: **Miguel de Cervantes, Spanish writer,** *Don Quixote*, **from the preface, 1605**

...a satire of knight-errantry ... the fall and destruction of that monstrous heap of ill-contrived romances ... which have so strangely infatuated the greater part of mankind.

Document E

> SOURCE: **Miguel de Cervantes, Spanish writer, *Don Quixote*, Sancho speaking, 1605**
>
> Everyone is as God made him, and often worse.

Document F

> SOURCE: **From an old Spanish tale, circa 1620**
>
> [Philip III] standing one day on the balcony of the palace at Madrid, observed a student, with a book in his hand, on the opposite bank of the Manzanares. He was reading, but every now and then he interrupted his reading and gave himself violent blows upon the forehead, accompanied with innumerable motions of ecstasy and mirthfulness. "That student," said the King, "is either out of his wits or reading … Don Quixote."

Document G

> SOURCE: **Lope Félix de Vega Carpio, Spanish poet, *The Star of Seville*, 1623**
>
> Arias: The one who threw roses to you is Dona Mencia Coronél.
>
> King: A handsome dame, but I saw others lovelier. … One I saw there full of grace, whom you have left unmentioned. … Who is she who on her balcony drew my attention, and to whom I doffed my hat? Who is she whose two eyes flashed lightning like Jove's thunderbolts and sent their deadly rays into my heart? …
>
> Arias: Her name is Dona Stella Tabera, and Seville in homage calls her its star.
>
> King: And it might call her its sun. … O vision that inflames my inmost soul!

Document H

SOURCE: **Pedro Calderón de la Barca, Spanish poet,** *The Monstrous Magician,* **1637**

So beautiful she was—and I,

Between my love and jealousy,

Am so convulsed with hope and fear,

Unworthy as it may appear—

So bitter is the life I live,

That—hear me, Hell!—I now would give

To thy most detested spirit

My soul, forever to inherit,

To suffer punishment and pine,

So that this woman may be mine.

3. MOZART

Exercise Question: Mozart is sometimes credited with synthesizing all that was the Enlightenment, and simultaneously starting the Romantic Movement in music. To what extent can the music and ideas of Wolfgang Amadeus Mozart be seen as a reaction to, rather than a synthesis of, Enlightenment thought?

Document A

SOURCE: **Jean Jacques Rousseau, French Enlightenment philosophe,** *Émile,* **May 1762**

...what I feel to be right is right, what I feel to be wrong is wrong. ... Too often does reason deceive us; we have only too good a right to doubt her... .

Document B

SOURCE: **Johann Gottfried Herder German philosopher,** *Treatise on the Ode,* **1765**

The more the teachings of all philosophy approach experience and the subjective categories of being, the more certain they indeed become… aesthetics altogether is closely akin to our heart, as it deals with the most delicate experiences of sensibility rather than general principles of reason…

Document C

SOURCE: **Wolfgang Amadeus Mozart, in a letter to his father, June 12, 1778**

The human voice is naturally tremulous, but only so far as to be beautiful; such is the nature of the voice, and it is imitated not only on wind instruments, but on stringed instruments, and even on the piano. But the moment the proper boundary is passed it is no longer beautiful, because it becomes unnatural.

Document D

SOURCE: **Johann Wolfgang von Goethe, German playwright,** *Faust: A Tragedy,* **1787**

O woe! woe which no human soul can grasp, that more than one being should sink into the depths of this misery, – that the first, in its writhing death-agony under the eyes of the Eternal Forgiver, did not expiate the guilt of all others! The misery of this single one pierces to the very marrow of my life; and thou art calmly grinning at the fate of thousands.

Document E

SOURCE: **Wolfgang Amadeus Mozart, *Don Giovanni*, Don Giovanni speaking as he is pulled into hell, 1787**

My soul is rent in agony!

Condemn'd to endless misery,

Oh, doom of wrath and terror,

No more to see the light!

Document F

SOURCE: **Wolfgang Amadeus Mozart, source unknown**

Neither a lofty degree of intelligence nor imagination nor both together go to the making of genius. Love, love, love, that is the soul of genius.

Document G

SOURCE: **Franz Niemetschek, Czech philosopher, Review of Mozart's *Tito* performed at Prague, 1794**

There is a certain Grecian simplicity, a quiet sublimity, in the entire music that strike a sensitive heart gently yet all the more deeply; these qualities fit the character of Tito, the times, and the entire subject so well that they do honor to Mozart's delicate taste and his powers of observation. At the same time the cantilena ... is of a heavenly sweetness, full of emotion and expression; the choruses are stately and sublime... .

4. ART OF REVOLUTION

Exercise Question: *Analyze the extent to which the art of the late 18th and early 19th centuries reflected the spirit of the French Revolution.*

Document A

SOURCE: **Johann Joachim Winckelmann, German art historian,** *History of Ancient Art,* **1764**

… the principal and universal characteristic of the masterpieces of Greek art is a noble simplicity and a quiet grandeur. … As the depth of the sea remains always at rest, however, the surface may be agitated, so the expression in the figures of the Greeks reveals in the midst of passion a great and steadfast soul.

Document B

SOURCE: **Jacques-Louis David, French painter,** *The Death of Socrates,* **1787**

Document C

SOURCE: Jacques-Louis David, French painter, *Bonaparte Crossing the St. Bernard Pass*, 1801

Document D

SOURCE: **Charles Percier and Pierre F. L. Fontaine, French architects,** *Arc de Triomphe du Carrousel,* **Paris, 1806**

Document E

SOURCE: Alexandre-Pierre Vignon, French architect, La Madeleine, Paris, 1806–1852

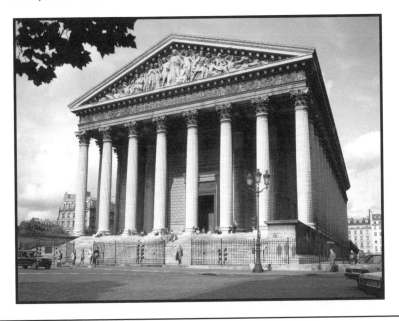

Document F

SOURCE: Jane Austen, English novelist, *Sense and Sensibility*, 1811

Elinor, this eldest daughter whose advice was so effectual, possessed a strength of understanding, and coolness of judgment, which qualified her, though only nineteen, to be the counsellor of her mother ... Marianne's abilities were, in many respects, quite equal to Elinor's. She was sensible and clever, but eager in everything; her sorrows, her joys, could have no moderation. She was generous, amiable, interesting: she was everything but prudent.

Document G

SOURCE: **Ferdinand Ries, German composer,** *Biography of Ludwig von Beethoven*, **1838**

In writing this symphony Beethoven had been thinking of Buonaparte, but Buonaparte while he was First Consul. At that time Beethoven had the highest esteem for him and compared him to the greatest consuls of ancient Rome. Not only I, but many of Beethoven's closer friends, saw this symphony on his table, beautifully copied in manuscript, with the word "Buonaparte" inscribed at the very top of the title-page and "Ludwig van Beethoven" at the very bottom. … I was the first to tell him the news that Buonaparte had declared himself Emperor, whereupon he broke into a rage and exclaimed, "So he is no more than a common mortal! Now, too, he will tread under foot all the rights of man, indulge only his ambition; now he will think himself superior to all men, become a tyrant!" Beethoven went to the table, seized the top of the title-page, tore it in half and threw it on the floor. The page had to be re-copied and it was only now that the symphony received the title "Sinfonia eroica."

5. ART OF THE ROMANTIC ERA

Exercise Question: *In what ways did Romanticism differ from the Baroque tradition that preceded it?*

Document A

SOURCE: **Jean Jacques Rousseau, French philosopher,** *Heloise*, **1761**

I consider all dramatic authors corruptors of the people. … [Novelists ought to] lead all back to nature; to give to men a love for a simple and egalitarian life; to cure them of the whims of opinion, restoring to them a taste for real pleasures; to make them love solitude and peace; to hold them at some distance from one another; and, in place of arousing them to crowd into towns, to incline them to spread themselves equally over the land, to vitalize it from all sides.

Document B

> SOURCE: **Johann Wolfgang von Goethe, German playwright,** *Faust: A Tragedy,* **1787**
>
> … crowd and jostle, whirl, and flutter!
>
> They whisper, babble, twirl, and splutter!
>
> They glimmer, sparkle, stink, and flare—
>
> A true witch-element! Beware!

Document C

> SOURCE: **Lord Byron, English Romantic poet, his translation of the famous** *Greek War Song,* **1811**
>
> Sons of the Greeks! Let us go
>
> In arms against the foe. …
>
> Then mutually despising
>
> The Turkish tyrant's yoke,
>
> Let your country see you rising,
>
> And all her chains are broke.

Document D

SOURCE: **Francisco Goya, Spanish painter,** *Executions of the Third of May, 1808*, 1814–1815

Document E

SOURCE: Théodore Géricault, French artist, detail of *Raft of the "Medusa,"* 1819

Document F

SOURCE: Victor Hugo, French writer, "Witches' Sabbath," from *Odes et Ballades*, 1826

All in unison moving with swift-circling feet

While Satan keeps time with his crozier's beat,

And their steps shake the arches colossal and high,

Disturbing the dead in their tombs close by.

Document G

SOURCE: **François-Joseph Fétis, nineteenth-century music critic, about Berlioz's *Symphonie fantastique***

The fifth part, the Dream of a Witches' Sabbath, mingles the trivial, the grotesque, and the barbarous; it is a saturnalia of noise and not of music. The pen falls from my hand.

6. POST-ROMANTIC REALISM

Exercise Question: List and analyze the characteristics of the works of Realism produced in the 19th century.

Document A

SOURCE: **Honore de Balzac, French author, *The Human Comedy*, 1842**

Each story presented some singularity; on the first floor four tall, narrow windows, close together, were filled as to the lower panes with boards, so as to produce the doubtful light by which a clever salesman can ascribe to his goods the color his customers inquire for. The young man seemed very scornful of this part of the house; his eyes had not yet rested on it. The windows of the second floor, where the Venetian blinds were drawn up, revealing little dingy muslin curtains behind the large Bohemian glass panes, did not interest him either. His attention was attracted to the third floor, to the modest sash-frames of wood, so clumsily wrought that they might have found a place in the Museum of Arts and Crafts to illustrate the early efforts of French carpentry. These windows were glazed with small squares of glass so green that, but for his good eyes, the young man could not have seen the blue-checked cotton curtains which screened the mysteries of the room from profane eyes.

Document B

> **SOURCE: Gustave Courbet, French Realist artist, on being asked to paint angels in a church, 1861**
>
> I have never seen angels. Show me an angel and I'll paint one.

Document C

> **SOURCE: Émile Zola, French writer, "My Hates," 1866**
>
> I am little concerned with beauty or perfection. I don't care for the great centuries. All I care about is life, struggle, intensity. I am at ease in my generation.

Document D

> **SOURCE: Édouard Manet, French painter, *Portrait of Émile Zola*, 1868**
>
>

Document E

> SOURCE: **Edgar Degas, French artisit, letter to a friend from a visit to New Orleans, 1872**
>
> Everything attracts me here ... I look at everything.

Document F

> SOURCE: **Edgar Degas, French artist, *The Cotton Exchange at New Orleans*, 1873**
>
>

Document G

> SOURCE: **Henrick Ibsen, Norwegian playwright, *An Enemy of the People*, 1882**
>
> A man should never put on his best trousers when he goes out to battle for freedom and truth.

7. EXPRESSIONISM

Exercise Question: *Describe and analyze the views of Expressionism in the early 20th century.*

Document A

> **SOURCE:** from *Der Sturm*, **German Expressionist magazine, circa 1910**
>
> Expressionism is not a fashion. It is a view of the world; and a view by the senses, not by concepts. And at that, a view of the universe of which the earth is a part.

Document B

SOURCE: **Franz Marc, German Expressionist painter,** *The Tower of Blue Horses*, **1913**

Document C

> **SOURCE: Wassily Kandinsky, Russian-born French Expressionist artisit, writing of Expressionism in *Der blaue Reiter Almanac*, 1914**
>
> ...the question of form in art was of secondary importance, ... the question of art was principally one of content ... the inner element of the work, created by the vibration of the soul."

Document D

> **SOURCE: Franz Marc, German Expressionist painter, writing of Expressionists in the preface to *Der blaue Reiter Almanac*, 1914**
>
> We went with the divining rod through the art of the ages and of the present. We showed only that which was alive and untouched by the compulsion of conventions. Our love was dedicated to all in art that was born of itself, lives of itself, and does not walk on the crutches of convention. We pointed at any crack in the crust of convention, since we hoped for some power underneath which some day would come to light. . . . We set against great centuries a NO. We well know that by this simple NO we shall not interrupt the serious and methodical course of the sciences and of triumphant "progress." Nor do we intend to get ahead of this development, but we pursue a side-road—to the scornful astonishment of our contemporaries—which scarcely seems to be a road at all, and we say: This is the main road for the development of mankind.

Document E

> **SOURCE: Herwarth Walden, founder of *Der Sturm*, from *Der Sturm*, circa 1914**
>
> This apocalyptic time separates the poor people, who maintain that they know love, from those men who have love. It separates people who claim to know art from human beings who have art.

Document F

SOURCE: **Herwarth Walden, founder of *Der Sturm*, epitaph to Franz Marc, 1916**

The animals listened to him, and he gave them the colors of his love. / The love of his colors. How they love each other, the colors, if one does not disturb them. How the forms embrace if one does not break them. / No fire burns those who themselves are burning.

Document G

SOURCE: **Kasimir Edschmid, German author, from "On poetic expressionism," 1917**

A good impressionist is a greater artist and has more chance to live in eternity than the mediocre creation of the expressionist looking for immortality. Zola's shameless, gigantic, stuttering, naked power will perhaps better stand the tribunal of the day of judgment than our great wrestling with God. But this, too, is fate.

Document H

SOURCE: **Rudolf Blümner, actor, from *The Spirit of Cubism and the Arts*, 1921**

It is easy to understand my great delight when I read in him [Thomas Aquinas]: the species impressa is a matter for sinful man, the species expressa is for the angels and for souls freed from the body.

8. POSTMODERNISM

Exercise Question: *Identify and analyze the characteristics of postmodernism in art and philosophy.*

Document A

SOURCE: **Lionel Trilling, literary critic from** *The Liberal Imagination: Essays on Literature and Society,* **1950.**

The educated classes are learning to blame ideas for our troubles, rather than blaming what is a very different thing—our own bad thinking. This is the great vice of academicism, that it is concerned with ideas rather than with thinking, and nowadays the errors of academicism do not stay in the academy; they make their way into the world, and what begins as a failure of perception among intellectual specialists finds its fulfillment in policy and action.

Document B

SOURCE: **H. Foster, from "Re: Post" in** *Art after Modernism,* **1984.**

No matter how "transcendental" or radically new the art, it is usually recouped, rendered familiar by historicism. Late modernism only reworks the contradiction: art is avant-garde insofar as it is radically historicist— the artist delves into art historical conventions in order to break out of them. Such historicism (the New as its own Tradition) is both an origin and an end for the avant-garde; and one aim for postmodernism is to retain its radicality but be rid of its historicism.

Document C

> **SOURCE: Abigail Solomon-Godeau, art historian, from "Photography after Art Photography," in *Art after Modernism*, 1984.**
>
> Virtually every critical and theoretical issue which postmodernist art may be said to engage in in one sense or another can be located with photography [and computer art]. Issues having to do with authorship, subjectivity, and uniqueness are built into the very nature of the photographic [and computer] process itself.

Document D

> **SOURCE: Michael Dear, from "The postmodern challenge: reconstructing human geography," 1988**
>
> . . . the notion that one has to choose between modernism and postmodernism is itself a highly modernist stance.

Document E

> **SOURCE: Zygmunt Bauman, Polish sociologist, from *Imitations of Postmodernity*, 1992**
>
> [The group is] unable to override the diversity of its supporters' interests and thus claim and secure their total allegiance and identification.

Document F

> **SOURCE: Keith Jenkins, British historian, from *On "What is History?"*, 1995**
>
> [An] historical work is a verbal artifact, a narrative prose discourse, the content of which is as much invented—or as much imagined—as found.

Document G

> SOURCE: **Fredric Jameson, literary critic, from *The Cultural Turn: Selected Writings on the Postmodern, 1993–1998*, 1998**
>
> [Postmodernism is a] concept whose function is to correlate the emergence of new formal features in culture with the emergence of a new type of social life and new economic order.

Part C—Analytical Transitions

Directions: For each of the following exercises, you will continue to practice all the skills covered so far in this book:

Step 1: Identify the tasks and terms

Step 2: Brainstorm specific evidence (and analyze the documents in the DBQ)

Step 3: Develop a thesis and categories of evidence, and then outline your argument

Step 4: Write an opening paragraph

Step 5: Analyze your specific evidence in three body paragraphs

Then, using the example from the handbook as a model, write transition sentences to analytically connect the ideas within your body paragraphs. Remember that transitions are not simply exercises in good writing style, but can be effective tools of analysis as well. Your transitions should connect the main ideas of your argument.

1. COLUMBIAN EXCHANGE

Exercise Question: To what extent was the Columbian Exchange mutually beneficial to Native Americans and Europeans?

Document A

SOURCE: **Pope Paul III, in a decree, 1537**

...all Indians are truly men, not only capable of understanding the Catholic faith, but ... exceedingly desirous to receive it.

Document B

SOURCE: **Domingo Martínez de Irala, first governor of Paraguay, message left for his successor, 1542**

In one of the islands of San Gabriel a sow and a boar have been left to breed. Do not kill them. If there should be many, take those you need, but always leave some to breed, and also, on your way, leave a sow and a boar on the island of Martin Garcia and on the other islands wherever you think it good, so that they may breed.

Document C

SOURCE: **Anonymous aborigine of Yucatan, speaking of pre-Spanish life, circa 1550**

There was then no sickness; they had no aching bones; they had then no high fever; they had then no smallpox; they had then no burning chest; they had then no abdominal pain; they had then no consumption; they had then no headache. At that time the course of humanity was orderly. The foreigners made it otherwise when they arrived here.

Document D

> SOURCE: **Thomas Hariot, naturalist, writing of his voyage to Roanoke colony, 1585**
>
> ... within a few days after our departure . . . people began to die very fast, and many in short space; in some towns about twenty, in some forty, in some sixty, & in one six score, which in truth was very many in respect to their numbers. ... The disease was also so strange that they neither knew what it was, nor how to cure it; the like by report of the oldest men in the country never happened before... .

Document E

> SOURCE: **John Gerard, English plant expert,** *Herball, Generall Historie of Plants,* **1597**
>
> We have as yet no certain proof or experience concerning the virtues of this kind of Corn, although the barbarous Indians which know no better are constrained to make a virtue of necessity, and think it a good food: whereas we may easily judge that it nourishes but little, and is of a hard and evil digestion, a more convenient food for swine than for man.

Document F

> SOURCE: **Anonymous German missionary to the New World, 1699**
>
> ...the Indians die so easily that the bare look and smell of a Spaniard causes them to give up the ghost.

Document G

> SOURCE: **Anonymous German missionary to the New World, 1699**
>
> A Comanche on his feet is out of his element, and comparatively almost as awkward as a monkey on the ground, without a limb or a branch to cling to; but the moment he lays his hand upon his horse, his face even becomes handsome, and he gracefully flies away like a different being.

2. APPLICATIONS OF DIVINE RIGHT THEORY

Exercise Question: Compare and contrast the applications of divine right theory in France and England during the 17ᵗʰ century.

3. SKEPTICISM AND WITCHCRAFT

Exercise Question: Identify and analyze the arguments for and against the existence of witchcraft 1500–1800.

Document A

Source: **Pope Alexander VI, from the papal bull *Cum acceperimus*, 1501**

Since we have learned that in the province of Lombardy many people of both sexes give themselves over to diverse incantations and devilish superstitions in order to procure many wicked things by their venery [sexual] and vain rites, to destroy men, beasts, and fields, to spread great scandal, and to induce grievous errors, we decree, in order both to fulfill our pastoral office from our high commission and to restrain these evils, scandals, and errors, that they shall cease. That is the reason why we send to you, commit to you, and order you and your successors appointed in Lombardy our full confidence in the Lord, that you may seek out diligently those people of both sexes (either by yourself or with the aid of a company which you shall choose) and secure and punish them through the medium of justice.

Document B

> SOURCE: **Reginald Scot, *The Discoverie of Witchcraft*, 1584**
>
> Excommunicated persons, partakers of the fault, infants, wicked servants, and runaways are to be admitted to bear witness against their dames in this matter of witchcraft: because (says Bodin the champion of witchmongers) none that be honest are able to detect them. Heretics also and witches shall be received to accuse, but none to excuse a witch. And finally, the testimony of all infamous persons in this case is good and allowed. Yea, one lewd person (says Bodin) may be received to accuse and condemn a thousand suspected witches.

Document C

> SOURCE: **Michel de Montaigne, "Concerning Cripples," 1588**
>
> The witches of my neighborhood are in mortal danger every time some new author comes along and attests to the reality of their visions. ... He who imposes his argument by bravado and command shows that it is weak in reason. ... To kill men, we should have sharp and luminous evidence . ... My ears are battered by a thousand stories like this: "Three people saw him on such-and-such a day in the east; three saw him the next day in the west... ." Truly, I would not believe my own self about this. How much more natural and likely it seems to me that two men are lying than that one man should pass with the winds in twelve hours from the east to the west! How much more natural that our understanding should be carried away from its base by the volatility of our untracked mind than that one of us, in flesh and bone, should be wafted up a chimney on a broomstick by a strange spirit!

Document D

> SOURCE: **Salazar Frias, Spanish inquisitor, from a dissenting verdict in a trial, 1610**
>
> ...if, for instance, we take the evidence of witnesses against Juan de la Bastida (alias Lambert), there are some who maintain they have seen him at the aquelarre [witch's Sabbath] on the selfsame days and times when he was under lock and key in the Tribunal's secret prison. ... Neither have definite proofs been produced by the things that outside witnesses have been brought to confirm, concerning the witches' assemblies, the ointment... .

Document E

> SOURCE: **Salazar Frias, Spanish inquisitor, from his proposals to the *Suprema* of the Inquisition, 1614**
>
> The Tribunal is to publish an edict imposing silence regarding the whole question of witchcraft. Any person whose conscience may be troubling him in connection with these matters is to be enjoined not to discuss his problem with others but to go straight to one of the commissioners or to his own confessor, who can communicate the matter to the Tribunal. The same discretion is to be observed by persons who wish to accuse others of witchcraft.

Document F

> SOURCE: **Friedrich Spee, from *Precautions for Prosecutors*, 1631**
>
> And so, as soon as possible, she is hurried to the torture, if indeed she be not subjected to it on the very day of her arrest, as often happens. For in these trials there is granted to nobody an advocate or any means of fair defense ... and whoever ventures to defend the prisoner is brought into suspicion of the crime as are all those who dare to utter a protest in these cases and to urge the judges to caution; for they are forthwith dubbed patrons of the witches.

Document G

> **SOURCE: Thomas Hobbes, from *Leviathan*, 1651**
>
> …I find in Scripture that there be Angels, and Spirits, good and evil … but not that any man's body was possessed, or inhabited by them… . Nevertheless, the contrary Doctrine … hath hitherto so prevailed in the Church, that the use of Exorcism, is thereupon built … That there were many Demonic in the Primitive Church, and few Madmen … whereas in these times we hear of, and see many Mad-men, and few Demonic, proceeds not from the change of Nature; but of Names.

Document H

> **SOURCE: Balthasar Bekker, from *The World Bewitched*, 1691**
>
> There is no argument so absurd as that of attributing an unusual effect to an occult or unknown cause … I have not thumbed through books in such a way that there could not be in them certain things formerly known to be natural things, but that pass today for witchcraft.

4. ROBESPIERRE AS AN IDEALIST

Exercise Question: To what extent was the French Revolutionary, Maximilien Robespierre, an idealistic proponent of Enlightenment ideas?

5. THE BOER WAR

Exercise Question: *Analyze the ways in which the Boer War was portrayed in published works.*

Document A

SOURCE: **Richard Harding Davis, from** *With Both Armies in South Africa*, **1900**

Just as they had reached the centre of the town, General Sir George White and his staff rode down from headquarters and met the men whose coming meant for him life and peace and success. They were advancing at a walk, with the cheering people hanging to their stirrups, clutching at their hands and hanging to the bridles of their horses.

General White's first greeting was characteristically unselfish and loyal, and typical of the British officer. He gave no sign of his own incalculable relief, nor did he give to Caesar the things which were Caesar's. He did not cheer Dundonald, nor Buller, nor the column which had rescued him and his garrison from present starvation and probable imprisonment at Pretoria. He raised his helmet and cried, "We will give three cheers for the Queen!" And then the General and the healthy ragged and sunburned troopers from the outside world, the starved, fever-ridden garrison and the starved, fever-ridden civilians stood with hats off and sang their national anthem.

The column outside had been fighting steadily for six weeks to get Dundonald or any one of its force into Ladysmith; for fourteen days it had been living in the open, fighting by night as well as by day, without halt or respite; the garrison inside had been for four months holding the enemy at bay with the point of the bayonet; it was famished for food, it was rotten with fever, and yet when the relief came and all turned out well, the first thought of everyone was for the Queen!

Document B

> **SOURCE: from a news article in *The Guardian*, March 2, 1900**
>
> To describe with any degree of adequacy the excitement in London, and indeed throughout the country, consequent upon the announcement yesterday of the relief of Ladysmith would be an almost impossible task. The news was made known a few minutes before ten o'clock at the War Office, and soon after the hour the welcome intelligence was proclaimed by the Lord Mayor from a window of the Mansion House.

Document C

> **SOURCE: H.W. Wilson, from *With the Flag to Pretoria, A History of the Boer War, 1899–1900*, 1901**
>
> The Boer scouts stealthily watched him, crawling through the thick bush in which a stranger without his bearings is as helpless as a ship without compass on the trackless ocean, and, on the information which they gave, Cronje marched swiftly north, and a second time placed himself on the British line of advance. Already runners had come in to the British camp from the north. One, from the brave and steadfast Colonel Plumer, announced that that officer would effect his junction with Mahon north-west of Mafeking; the other, from Colonel Baden-Powell, asked for information as to the numbers, guns, and supplies of the column.
>
> Such information was not lightly to be entrusted to any messenger; there was no cipher of which Baden-Powell had the key; but in these straits, Colonel Rhodes, the intelligence officer with the column, succeeded in inventing a most ingenious reply, unintelligible to the Boers, but clear as daylight to the British. It is thus given by Mr. Filson Young: "Our numbers are the Naval and Military multiplied by ten; our guns, the number of sons in the Ward family; our supplies, the officer commanding the 9th Lancers." The key to the message was that there were 940 men, 94 Piccadilly being the number of the Naval and Military Club; that the guns were six, that being the number of sons in the house of Dudley; and that the supplies were little.

Document D

> SOURCE: **from a news article in** *The Guardian*, **June 2, 1902**
>
> The announcement of peace was made at the evening service at St. Paul's Cathedral to a fairly large congregation. . . . The Bishop of Stepney then ascended the pulpit and said: "I desire to announce to the congregation that God has been pleased to answer our prayers and to give us the blessings of peace." He added: "I will read to you the telegram which has been sent by the Commander-in-Chief to the Secretary of State for War." Having done this he proceeded: "Comment is needless, but I ask you to offer your heartfelt thanks to Almighty God by singing instead of the hymn on the paper another hymn suitable to the occasion, and to follow that by singing to the occasion, and to follow that by singing two verses of the National Anthem." The hymn referred to was "Now thank we all our God," and the congregation sang it with much feeling and impressiveness.

Document E

> SOURCE: **Arthur Conan Doyle,** *The Great Boer War,* **1902**
>
> Monday, October 30th, 1899, is not a date which can be looked back to with satisfaction by any Briton. In a scrambling and ill-managed action we had lost our detached left wing almost to a man, while our right had been hustled with no great loss but with some ignominy into Ladysmith. Our guns had been outshot, our infantry checked, and our cavalry paralysed. Eight hundred prisoners may seem no great loss when compared with a Sedan, or even with an Ulm; but such matters are comparative, and the force which laid down its arms at Nicholson's Nek is the largest British force which has surrendered since the days of our great grandfathers, when the egregious Duke of York commanded in Flanders.

Document F

> SOURCE: **L. S. Amery,** *The Times History of the War in South Africa (1899–1902)*, **1902**
>
> The force Baden-Powell had with him was a mere handful—irregular mounted infantry, just learning to hold on to their saddles, Cape, Rhodesian, and Protectorate police, and a scratch selection of volunteers and town guard, with half-a-dozen antiquated little muzzleloaders for artillery—but animated with a spirit of confidence in themselves, and in the courage and resourcefulness of their leader, that was to prove of more worth than numbers or training, or batteries of field artillery, and to frustrate Cronje's hopes and the whole Boer plan of campaign in the west.

Document G

> SOURCE: **C. R. B. Barrett, from** *History of the XIII Hussars*, **1910**
>
> About 2 A.M. on the 16th a party of Boers came down to Klippoortiie, a place about a mile and a half outside Heidelberg, and drove off a few cattle. The Kaffirs to whom it belonged stated that the enemy numbered about 200.
>
> On January 17, the South African Constabulary, whose camp was on the left of the 13th, began to form a depot at Heidelberg; and at Greylingstad and Waterval detachments were similarly employed.
>
> January 23, 1901. An official announcement of the death of Her Majesty Queen Victoria was received.
>
> A telegram concerning the accession of His Majesty King Edward VII was received by Lord Kitchener three days later. This contained a message to the army in South Africa, which was duly communicated to the troops. A loyal and dutiful reply was forwarded by his lordship conveying the devotion of the troops to the King.

Document H

> SOURCE: **Sir Baden-Powell, from** *Lessons from the Varsity of Life*, **1933**
>
> My orders were to raise two battalions of Mounted Rifles, to mount, equip, train, and supply them, with the least possible delay and the least possible display.
>
> … Also, I was to take charge of and organise the Police of Rhodesia and Bechuanaland as part of my force.
>
> But I was to make as little show as possible of these preparations for fear of precipitating war by arousing the animosity of the Boers.
>
> The object of my force and its establishment on the north-west border of the Transvaal was, in the event of war, to attract Boer forces away from the coast so that they should not interfere with the landing of British troops: secondly, to protect our possessions in Rhodesia and Mafeking, etc. Thirdly, to maintain British prestige among the great native tribes in those parts.

6. GERMAN AMBITIONS AND WORLD WAR I

Exercise Question: *Identify the goals of Germany at the start of World War I. To what extent were these ambitions responsible for the war?*

7. SCIENCES IN POST-WWII SOVIET RUSSIA

Exercise Question: *Describe and analyze the role of the Soviet political system, under Stalin, in determining the success or failure of Soviet scientists and shaping Soviet scientific theory.*

Document A

SOURCE: **Joseph Stalin, in conversation with popular writer, Konstantin Simonov, 1947**

...if you take our intelligentsia, scientific intelligentsia, professors, physicians—they are not sufficiently inculcated with the feeling of Soviet patriotism. They have unjustified admiration for foreign culture.

Document B

SOURCE: **B.F. Kedrov, Soviet philosopher of science, speaking of "self-criticism" in an address to a meeting of the Institute of Philosophy, January 1947**

... wait until your mistakes are repeated by someone else and then bravely, morally, and without fear criticize your own mistakes ... without mentioning your own name in the process.

Document C

SOURCE: **Andrei Zhdanov, in a speech for the "official" discussion of philosophy, June 1947**

The Kantian vagaries of modern bourgeois atomic physicists lead them to inferences about the electron's possessing "free will," the replacement of matter with some sort of collection of energy-bearing waves, and to other devilish tricks.

Document D

SOURCE: Joseph Stalin, letter of response to Trofim Lysenko, Fall 1947

Regarding the theoretical tenets in biology, I think that Michurin's tenet is the only scientific tenet. The Weismannists [opponents of Lamarckian theory] and their followers, who deny the inheritability of acquired characteristics, do not pay attention to what has been disseminated about them for a long time. ... the future belongs to Michurin.

Document E

SOURCE: Trofim Lysenko, letter to Joseph Stalin about a Yuri Zhdanov speech denouncing Lysenko's theories about "bourgeois biology," April 17, 1948

...[the] falsehoods of the anti-Michurinist neo-Darwinists will have much greater effect in the regions, both among scientific personnel and among agronomists and officials of practical farming, thereby strongly hindering the scientists under my direction from applying their results in practical farming. I turn to you, therefore, with a request that is very important to me: to help, if you consider it desirable to do so, in this matter that seems to me very serious for our agricultural science and biology.

Document F

SOURCE: Yuri Zhdanov, letter to Joseph Stalin, July 1948

The very organization of [my] report was wrong. I obviously failed to take into account my new position as an official of the Central Committee apparatus, underestimated my responsibility, and did not realize my presentation would be taken as the official stand of the Central Committee. ... My sharp and public criticism of Academician Lysenko was wrong. Academician Lysenko is now the recognized leader of the Michurinist school in biology, he has defended Michurin and his doctrine...

Document G

> SOURCE: **Artem Alikhanian, Soviet Armenian physicist, in speech to Soviet scientific apparatus, August 1948**
>
> From tomorrow on I shall not only myself, in all my scientific activity, try to emancipate myself from the old reactionary Weismann-Morganist views, I shall also try to reform and convince all my pupils and comrades. … And only in our country, the country with the most advanced and progressive world outlook, can the seedlings of the new scientific trend develop.

Document H

> SOURCE: **Joseph Stalin, published essay, Fall 1951**
>
> Marxism regards laws of science—whether they are laws of natural science or laws of political economy—as the reflection of objective processes which take place independently of the will of man.

8. SOVIET DECLINE AND UNIFICATION OF EUROPE

Exercise Question: *In what ways did the end of the Soviet Union invigorate the European unification movement?*

Effective Closing Paragraphs

Directions: For the following exercise, practice all the skills covered so far in this book.

Step 1: Identify the tasks and terms

Step 2: Analyze the documents and brainstorm specific evidence

Step 3: Develop a thesis and categories of evidence, and then outline your argument

Step 4: Write an opening paragraph

Step 5: Analyze your specific evidence in three body paragraphs and insert analytical transitions

Finally, write a closing paragraph for your essay. Remember that this final paragraph is your best opportunity to "stick the landing" in your essay. Summarize each part of your argument, alluding to your most significant evidence, and restate your thesis.

1. PROTESTANT AND CATHOLIC REFORMATION

Exercise Question: In what ways did the Protestant movement of the 16th century inspire reforms enacted within the Roman Catholic Church during the 17th century?

2. RUSSIAN TIME OF TROUBLES

Exercise Question: *Analyze the reasons for political instability during the Russian Time of Troubles.*

Document A

SOURCE: **An eyewitness account, 1603**

But I swear by God that in Moscow I saw, with my own eyes, people who rolled in the streets and, like animals, ate grass during the summer and hay during the winter. ... Human flesh, finely ground, baked in pies (a kind of pastry), was sold and consumed like beef. ... Daily, on the Tsar's orders they collected hundreds of corpses and carried them outside the city in wagons—an undertaking which was awesome to observe. Specially appointed people washed the dead, wrapped them in a white cloth, put red shoes on them, and wheeled them to the church to be buried.

Document B

SOURCE: **Gregory Otrepief, Russian monk and 1st "False Dimitri", to the people of Novgorod-Severski, 1604**

I am the Tzarevitch Dmitri, and I will not forget your kindness.

Document C

SOURCE: **Ivan Bolotnikov, to the Muscovites on the eve of the Siege of Moscow, November 1606**

If you do not surrender of your own free will, I and my lord [Tsar Dimitri] will do as we see fit and will soon visit ourselves upon you.

Document D

SOURCE: **Secretary Tomila, on being asked to open the gates of Smolensk to the Polish King Sigismond, 1609**

If I were to do it, not only would God and the Muscovites curse me, but the earth would open and swallow me. We are sent to negotiate in the interests of our country, not of ourselves.

Document E

SOURCE: **Anonymous Russian Boyar, upon the election of Michael Romanov as Tsar, 1613**

Let us have Misha Romanov for he is young and not yet wise; he will suit our purposes.

Document F

SOURCE: **Isaac Massa, Dutch grain trader, traveler, diplomat, and envoy to Russia, in his memoirs, 1614**

[Tsar Michael was surrounded by] young and ignorant men ... ravening wolves, who pluck and pillage the common people most of all.

Document G

SOURCE: **Gustavus Adolphus, Swedish king, seeking Russian alliance against Poland and the Catholic League, 1618**

When your neighbor's house is on fire you must bring water and try to extinguish it, to guarantee your own safety. May your Tzarian majesty help your neighbors to protect yourself.

Document H

SOURCE: **Duguay Cormenin, French ambassador to Russia, offering alliance against Poland, 1629**

His Tzarian majesty is the head of Eastern countries and the orthodox faith; Louis, King of France, is the head of Southern countries; and the Tzar, by contracting a friendship and alliance with him, will get the better of his enemies. As the Emperor is closely allied to the King of Poland, the Tzar must be allied to the King of France. These two princes are everywhere glorious; they have no equals either in strength or power; their subjects obey them blindly, while the English and Brabancons [Dutch] are only obedient when they choose. The latter buy their wares in Spain, and sell them to the Russians at a high price, but the French will furnish them with everything at a reasonable rate.

---

3. ROOTS OF DEISM

Exercise Question: *Identify the tenets of Deism and analyze their roots within the Scientific Revolution.*

4. SEARCH FOR LONGITUDE

Exercise Question: *Analyze and assess the various approaches suggested to solve the problem of determining longitude at sea.*

Document A

SOURCE: **King Charles II of England, charge to his first Astronomer Royal (John Flamsteed) in a warrant establishing the Royal Observatory at Greenwich, 1675**

…[apply] the most exact Care and Diligence to rectifying the Tables of the Motions of the Heavens, and the Places of the fixed Stars, so as to find out the so-much desired Longitude at Sea, for perfecting the art of Navigation.

Document B

SOURCE: **John Flamsteed, letter to his former assistant about the unauthorized publication of his star chart by Newton and Halley, 1712**

I committed them to the fire about a fortnight ago. … If Sir I. N. would be sensible of it, I have done both him and Dr. Halley a very great kindness.

Document C

SOURCE: **Jeremy Thacker, in response to the many fantastical ideas for a solution to the longitude problem, 1714**

In a word, I am satisfied that my Reader begins to think that the *Phonometers, Pyrometers, Selenometers, Heliometers,* and all the *Meters* are not worthy to be compared with my Chronometer.

Document D

> **SOURCE: Sir Isaac Newton, as a member of the Board of Longitude, letter to the secretary of the Admiralty, 1721**
>
> A good watch may serve to keep a reckoning at Sea for some days and to know the time of a celestial Observation: and for this end a good Jewel watch may suffice till a better sort of Watch can be found out. But when the Longitude at sea is once lost, it cannot be found again by any watch.

Document E

> **SOURCE: George Graham, Royal Society Fellow, endorsing Harrison's first sea clock, 1735**
>
> John Harrison, having with great labor and expense, contrived and executed a Machine for measuring time at sea, upon such Principle, as seem to us to Promise a very great and sufficient degree of Exactness. We are of Opinion, it highly deserves Public Encouragement, In order to a thorough Trial and Improvement, of the several Contrivances, for preventing those Irregularities in time, that naturally arise from the different degrees of Heat and Cold, a moist and dry Temperature of the Air, and the Various Agitations of the ship.

Document F

> **SOURCE: John Harrison, speaking of his fourth sea clock, known as "The Watch," 1759**
>
> I think I may make bold to say, that there is neither any other Mechanical or Mathematical thing in the World that is more beautiful or curious in texture than this my watch or Timekeeper for the Longitude ... and I heartily thank Almighty God that I have lived so long, as in some measure to complete it.

Document G

> SOURCE: **Captain James Cook, in his journal aboard the *Resolution*, 1772**
>
> I must here take note that indeed our error (in Longitude) can never be great, so long as we have so good a guide as [the] watch.

Document H

> SOURCE: **Alexander Dalrymple, East India Company, in *Some Notes Useful to Those Who Have Chronometers at Sea*, 1779**
>
> The machine used for measuring time at sea is here named chronometer, [as] so valuable a machine deserves to be known by a name instead of a definition.

5. VICTORIAN SOCIETY

Exercise Question: *Identify and analyze the social characteristics of Victorian England.*

6. BREST-LITOVSK NEGOTIATIONS

Exercise Question: *Analyze the reasons for and responses to Russia's withdrawal from World War I in 1917.*

Document A

SOURCE: **Second All-Russian Congress of Soviets, Peace Resolution, November 10, 1917**

The Government considers a peace to be democratic and equitable which is aspired to by a majority of the working classes of all the belligerent countries. ... It should be an immediate peace, without annexation, (that is to say, without usurpation of foreign territory, and without violent conquest of nationalities,) and without indemnities...

Document B

SOURCE: **Leon Trotsky, Russian Commissar for Foreign Affairs, note sent to the Entente and American Embassies at Petrograd, November 20, 1917**

...the Congress of Workmen's, Soldiers' and Peasants' Delegates of All the Russias, instituted on November 8 a new Government of the Republic of All the Russias ... [and approved] proposals for a truce and for a democratic peace without annexation and without indemnities, based on the principle of the independence of nations and of their right to determine for themselves the nature of their own development.

Document C

> **SOURCE: Lord Robert Cecil, Parliamentary Under-Secretary of State for Foreign Affairs, November 23, 1917**
>
> The action just taken by the extremists in Petrograd ... would of course be a direct breach of the agreement of September 5, 1914, and ... if approved and adopted by the Russian nation would put them practically outside the pale of the ordinary councils of Europe. But I do not believe that the Russian people will confirm this action or approve a proclamation ... to open all along the line peace negotiations with the enemy across the trenches. ... There is no intention of recognizing such a Government.

Document D

> **SOURCE: General Lavergne, head of the French mission at the Russian Staff Headquarters, November 27, 1917**
>
> France does not recognize the power of the People's Commissars. Trusting in the patriotism of the Russian High Command it counts upon the firm resolution of the military leaders to repel every criminal pourparler and to keep the Russian army facing the common enemy. Besides, I am charged to call your attention to the fact that the question of an armistice is a governmental question, whose discussion cannot be taken up without previous consent of the Allied Governments. No Government has the right to discuss separately the question of an armistice or of peace.

Document E

> **SOURCE: Major Kerth, Military Attache at Petrograd, November 27, 1917**
>
> Acting by virtue of instructions received from my Government and transmitted through the Ambassador of the United States at Petrograd, I have the honor to bring to your knowledge the fact that the United States, an ally of Russia, pursuing with her the war which is the struggle of democracy against autocracy, protests energetically and categorically against any separate armistice that might be concluded by Russia.

Document F

> **SOURCE: Count Czernin, Foreign Minister of the Austro-Hungarian Government, wire to the Russian Government, November 29, 1917**
>
> …the guiding lines announced by the Russian Government for negotiations for an armistice and a treaty of peace, counter proposals to which are awaited by the Russian Government, are, in the opinion of the Austro-Hungarian Government, a suitable basis for entering into these negotiations … regarding an immediate armistice and general peace.

Document G

> **SOURCE: von Kuehlmann, German Foreign Secretary, address to the Main Committee of the Reichstag, November 30, 1917**
>
> Russia has set the world ablaze. … Russia has swept away the culprits, and she is laboring to find through an armistice and peace an opportunity for her internal reconstruction. … The principles announced to the world by the present rulers in Petrograd appear to be entirely acceptable as a basis for the reorganization of affairs in the East—a reorganization which, while fully taking into account the right of nations to determine their own destinies, is calculated permanently to safeguard the essential interests of the two great neighboring nations, Germany and Russia.

Document H

> **SOURCE: Leon Trotsky, to the Allied nations, November 30, 1917**
>
> The Government cannot permit Allied diplomatic and military agents to interfere in the internal affairs of our country and attempt to incite civil war.

7. SOVIET OPPOSITION IN EASTERN EUROPE

Exercise Question: *To what extent were the opposition movements in Eastern Europe 1950–1988 successful in breaking down Soviet domination of the region?*

8. 21ST-CENTURY ENVIRONMENTAL CHALLENGES

Exercise Question: *Analyze the ways in which economic policy interacts with environmental policy in the 21st century.*

Document A

SOURCE: Stephen Harper, Canadian Prime Minister, remarks at the UN Climate Summit, September 25, 2007

The core principle of Canada's approach to climate change is balance. …
We are balancing environmental protections with economic growth.

Document B

SOURCE: Angela Merkel, German Chancellor, remarks at the UN Climate Summit, September 25, 2007

By the middle of this century, we need to at least halve global emissions.

Document C

> SOURCE: **Ban Ki-moon, United Nations Secretary General, closing remarks at the UN Climate Summit, September 25, 2007**
>
> We need to ensure that such an agreement is in force by 2012. … undoubtedly there is a need for much deeper emission reductions from industrialized countries. … The cost of inaction will far outweigh the cost of action. … The current level of effort will not suffice.

Document D

> SOURCE: **Georg Kell, Executive Director, United Nations Global Compact, in an op-ed article entitled "Climate Change: Is Business Doing Enough?" February 23, 2009**
>
> …business must flex its advocacy muscle and push even more companies to take action on climate change—within their sectors, their markets, down their supply chains. Likewise, business should use its influence with policy makers to lobby for carbon reductions and workable technical standards. What we really need is [a] new era of business statesmanship driven by the realization that the time to act is now.

Document E

> SOURCE: **Yvo de Boer, United Nations Climate Chief, speaking with a newspaper about the need for a treaty from the international climate conference in Copenhagen, March 16, 2009**
>
> I get the impression talking to business people that they still want clarity from Copenhagen. If you're making investments now, for example in the energy sector, in power plants that are going to be around for the next 30 to 50 years, you can't really afford to keep waiting and waiting and waiting for governments to say where they're going to go on this issue.

Document F

SOURCE: Connie Hedegaard, Danish Minister for Climate and Energy, quote from anews interview, October 2, 2009

If the whole world comes to Copenhagen and leaves without making the needed political agreement, then I think it's a failure that is not just about climate. Then it's the whole global democratic system not being able to deliver results in one of the defining challenges of our century. And that is and should not be a possibility. It's not an option.

Document G

SOURCE: News article entitled "The Czech Republic makes big money through carbon trading," October 2, 2009

Under the Kyoto Protocol, the Czech Republic is committed to reducing its carbon emissions by eight percent from 1990 levels by 2012. ... So far, it has already cut them by 24 percent owing to industrial restructuring and other measures, giving the government 140 million units of carbon credits to sell...

Document H

SOURCE: Yu Qingtai, Chinese climate envoy, quote from news interview, October 5, 2009

In my view, the fundamental reason for a lack of progress is the lack of political will on the part of Annex 1 [industrialized] countries.

The
Other
Question
Types

The New AP Multiple-Choice

Section 1: 1450–1648

Questions 1-2 refer to the documents that follow.

"Of Filippo Brunellesco, it may be said that he was given by heaven
to invest architecture with new forms, after it had wandered astray for
many centuries."

*Giorgio Vasari, Lives of the Most Eminent Painters,
Sculptors, and Architects, 1550*

Filippo Brunelleschi, dome of Santa Maria del Fiore, Florence, 1446

1. Which Renaissance value is best illustrated by the image above as well as Vasari's statement?

    a. Generalism

    b. Classicism

    c. Secularism

    d. Skepticism

2. Which of the following works BEST emphasizes the same value?

    a.

    b.

c.

d.

Section 2: 1648–1815

Questions 3-4 refer to the document that follows.

> "We are born capable of sensation and from birth are affected in diverse ways by the objects around us. As soon as we become conscious of our sensations we are inclined to seek or to avoid the objects which produce them: at first, because they are agreeable or disagreeable to us, later because we discover that they suit or do not suit us, and ultimately because of the judgments we pass on them by reference to the idea of happiness of perfection we get from reason. These inclinations extend and strengthen with the growth of sensibility and intelligence, but under the pressure of habit they are changed to some extent with our opinions. The inclinations before this change are what I call our nature. In my view everything ought to be in conformity with these original inclinations."

> **Jean Jacques Rousseau, French philosophe, Émile, May 1762**

3. Which of the following intellectual movements is most closely associated with the philosophy of Jean Jacques Rousseau as expressed in the document above?

   a. Christian Humanism

   b. Scientific Revolution

   c. Romanticism

   d. Irrationalism

4. Which of the following artists produced works influenced by ideas most closely related to those expressed in the document?

   a. William Blake

   b. Michelangelo Buonarroti

   c. Pablo Picasso

   d. Salvador Dali

Section 3: 1815–1914

Questions 5-6 refer to the document that follows.

"I have had 13 children, and have brought seven up. I have been accustomed to work in the fields at hay-time and harvest. Sometimes I have had my mother, and sometimes my sister, to take care of the children, or I could not have gone out. I have gone to work at seven in the morning till six in the evening; in harvest sometimes much later, but it depends on circumstances. Women with a family cannot be ready so soon as men, and must be home earlier, and therefore they don't work so many hours."

Mrs. Smart, from an interview in Reports of Special Assistant Poor Law Commissioners on the Employment of Women and Children in Agriculture, London, 1843

5. Which of the following historical eras is most closely associated with the document above?

   a. The Revolutions of 1848

   b. The Second Industrial Revolution

   c. The Romantic Period

   d. The English Revolution

6. Which of the following trends contributed most to the end of situations like that described in the document?

   a. Factory labor laws restricting the number of hours worked in a day

   b. Victorian cultural norms that emphasized the domesticity of women

   c. Poor laws aimed at caring for urban children in extreme poverty

   d. Suffragette movements that provided women with greater political power

Section 4: 1914–Present

Questions 7-8 refer to the document that follows.

"...at a time when climate change climbs to the top of the political agenda, wind energy continues to be the only advanced technology ready and able to deliver renewable power on a large scale. Cyprus is not among the windiest areas in the world, yet still we have a commitment to go to renewable energy, so we have to work harder than others."

Akis Ellinas, chairman of DK Wind Supply,
quoted in Utility Week, October 5, 2009

7. Which of the following events is most closely associated with the document above?

   a. The Copenhagen Summit

   b. The Oslo Accord

   c. The Kyoto Protocol

   d. The SALT II Agreement

8. The argument of Akis Ellinas in the document above is most similar to which of the following?

   a. A British MP arguing for a law to reduce carbon emissions in the UK

   b. A University of Milan professor arguing for more solar power research

   c. A Volvo CEO arguing for a computerized solution to better MPG

   d. An army general arguing for a military solution to a border crisis in Croatia

The Other Question Types

Short-Answer Questions

Section 1: 1450–1648

1. Use the passage below and your knowledge of European history to answer all parts of the question that follows.

    > "If you, with your nobles and the people of Constantinople accept the decree of union, you will find Us and Our venerable brothers, the cardinals of the Holy Roman Church, ever eager to support your honor and your empire. But if you and your people refuse to accept the decree, you will force Us to take such measures as are necessary for your salvation and Our honor."

    > *Pope Nicholas V to Constantine XI*
    > *(Byzantine Emperor), 1452*

    (A) Briefly identify and describe ONE cause of Pope Nicholas' demand for union.

    (B) Briefly identify and describe ONE result of Pope Nicholas' demand for union.

    (C) Briefly identify and describe how the Roman Catholic Church attempted to influence ONE European leader other than the Byzantine Emperor.

2. Use the passage below and your knowledge of European history to answer all parts of the question that follows.

"Ever since the commencement of the civil wars which are distracting the country, there has been a terrible change for the worse. So complete is the alteration, that those who knew France before would not recognize her again. Everywhere are to be seen shattered buildings, fallen churches, and towns in ruins; while the traveler gazes horror-stricken on spots which have of lately been the scenes of murderous deeds and inhuman cruelties."

Ogier Guiselin de Busbecq, Holy Roman Emperor's
Ambassador to France, from a letter, 1575

(A) Briefly identify and describe ONE cause of the events which led to the description above.

(B) Briefly identify and describe ONE result of the events which led to the description above.

(C) Briefly identify and describe how ONE country other than France experienced similar civil wars.

3. Answer all parts of the question.

Historians have argued that Protestantism did not become popular in England until the 1620s, well after Henry VIII's break with the Roman Catholic Church and Elizabeth's official imposition of Protestantism.

(A) Identify TWO pieces of evidence that support this argument and explain how each supports the argument.

(B) Identify ONE piece of evidence that undermines this argument and explain how the evidence undermines the argument.

4. Use the excerpts as well as your knowledge of European history to answer all parts of the question that follows.

"There was then no sickness; they had no aching bones; they had then no high fever; they had then no smallpox; they had then no burning chest; they had then no abdominal pain; they had then no consumption; they had then no headache. At that time the course of humanity was orderly. The foreigners made it otherwise when they arrived here."

Anonymous aborigine of Yucatan, from an interview, speaking of pre-Spanish life, circa 1550

"A Comanche on his feet is out of his element, and comparatively almost as awkward as a monkey on the ground, without a limb or a branch to cling to; but the moment he lays his hand upon his horse, his face even becomes handsome, and he gracefully flies away like a different being."

George Catlin, American painter, author, and traveler, 1841

(A) Briefly explain TWO economic developments that led to the situations shown in the two sources.

(B) Briefly explain ONE social development that led to the situations shown in the two sources.

Section 2: 1648–1815

5. Use the excerpt and the map as well as your knowledge of European history to answer both parts of the question that follows.

"If ever malice in concert with falsehood has been able to contrive a completely baseless rumor, it is assuredly the one which dares to imply that we have resolved to support a Piast [Polish noble with no blood line to the throne] for one purpose only, namely that, with his help, we could then easily invade several provinces of the Realm of Poland, dismember them, and appropriate them forthwith to Ourselves and Our Empire."

Catherine the Great, declaration to the courts of Europe disclaiming plans for a Partition, 1764

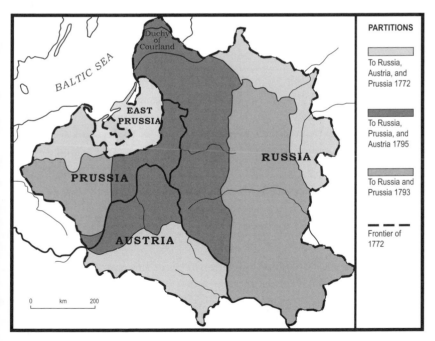

Salvatore Esposito, cartographer, The Partitions of Poland, 2010

(A) Briefly identify and describe TWO causes that might help to explain the connection between Catherine's declaration and the geopolitical changes illustrated in the map.

(B) Briefly identify and describe how ONE parallel event from another historical era.

6. Use the excerpt and your knowledge of European history to answer all parts of the question that follows.

"As the people had not appeared for a single instant on the public stage for a hundred and forty years, the possibility of their ever appearing there was forgotten, and their insensibility was regarded as a proof of deafness. Hence, when some interest began to be taken in their lot, they were discussed publically as though they had not been present. It appeared as though it was supposed that the discussion would only be heard by the upper classes, and that the only danger was lest these might not be made to understand the case.

The very classes which had most to fear from public fury declaimed loudly and publically against the cruel injustice which the people had so long suffered … Thus, in their endeavor to relieve the lower classes, they roused them to fury.

In the eighteenth century … it was disinterested principle and generous sympathy which roused the upper classes to revolution, while the people were agitated by the bitter feeling of their grievances, and a rage to change their condition. The enthusiasm of the former fanned the flame of popular wrath and covetousness, and ended by arming the people."

Alexis de Tocqueville, The Old Regime and the Revolution, 1856

(A) Provide ONE piece of evidence that supports Tocqueville's position.

(B) Provide ONE piece of evidence that undermines Tocqueville's position.

(C) Identify ONE example of any other revolution which contrasts with the description above.

7. Use the excerpts and your knowledge of European history to answer all parts of the question that follows.

"…This habitual restraint produces a docility which woman requires all her life long, for she will always be in subjection to a man, or a man's judgment, and she will never be free to set her own opinion above his. What is most wanted in a woman is gentleness. … A man, unless he is a perfect monster, will sooner or later yield to his wife's gentleness, and the victory will be hers.

Once it is demonstrated that men and women neither are, nor should be, constituted the same, either in character or in temperament, it follows that they should not have the same education. … Boys want movement and noise, drums, tops, toy-carts; girls prefer things which appeal to the eye, and can be used for dressing-up-mirrors, jewelry, finery, and specially dolls … The search for abstract and speculative truths for principles and axioms in science, for all that tends to wide generalizations, is beyond a woman's grasp."

Jean Jacques Rousseau, Emile, or On Education, _1762_

"What opinion are we to form of a system of education, when the author (Rousseau in Emile) says... 'Educate women like men, and the more they resemble our sex the less power will they have over us.' This is the very point I am at. I do not wish them to have power over men, but over themselves. The most perfect education, in my opinion, is … to enable the individual to attain such habits of virtue as will render it independent. In fact, it is a farce to call any being virtuous whose virtues do not result from the exercise of its own reason.

To be a good mother a woman must have sense, and that independence of mind which few women possess who are taught to depend entirely on their husbands. Meek wives are, in general, foolish mothers…

If children are to be educated to understand the true principle of patriotism, their mother must be a patriot … make women rational creatures, and free citizens, and they will quickly become good wives, and mothers; that is-if men do not neglect the duties of husbands and fathers."

Mary Wollstonecraft, A Vindication of the Rights of Women, _1792_

(A) Briefly explain TWO political developments that led to the debate highlighted by the two sources.

(B) Briefly explain ONE social development that led to the debate highlighted by the two sources.

8. Use the excerpt and your knowledge of European history to answer all parts of the question that follows.

[By the late 18th century] no longer could a "responsible" nurse hang her young swaddled charge on a hook and go about her own business. Instead, the care of the child became her primary business and, if Rousseau's vision became reality, the mother would become the ideal nurse, dispensing love and affection along with her breast-milk.

Jennifer J. Popiel, Associate Professor of History at St. Louis University, **Rousseau's Daughters: Domesticity, Education, and Autonomy in Modern France,** *2008.*

(A) Identify TWO pieces of evidence that connect the description above with the philosophy of Jean Jacques Rousseau and explain how each makes this connection.

(B) Identify ONE piece of evidence that undermines the connection between the description above and the philosophy of Jean Jacques Rousseau and explain how it undermines the connection.

Section 3: 1815–1914

9. Use the excerpt and your knowledge of European history to answer all parts of the question that follows.

"The events of the summer of 1848 in Prussia are soon told. The Constituent Assembly, or rather "the Assembly elected for the purpose of agreeing upon a Constitution with the Crown," and its majority of representatives of the middle class interest, had long since forfeited all public esteem by lending itself to all the intrigues of the Court, from fear of the more energetic elements of the population. They had confirmed, or rather restored, the obnoxious privileges of feudalism, and thus betrayed the liberty and the interests of the peasantry."

Karl Marx, from "Revolution and counter-revolution, or, Germany in 1848", article written April 17, 1852

(A) Identify TWO pieces of evidence that support this argument and explain how each supports the argument.

(B) Identify ONE piece of evidence that undermines this argument and explain how the evidence undermines the argument.

10. Use the excerpt and your knowledge of European history to answer all parts of the question that follows.

"Nature has placed mankind under the governance of two sovereign masters, pain and pleasure. It is for them alone to point out what we ought to do, as well as to determine what we shall do ... They govern us in all we do, in all we say, in all we think: every effort we can make to throw off our subjection, will serve but to demonstrate and confirm it.

...a principle, which lays down, as the only right and justifiable end of Government, the greatest happiness of the greatest number—how can it be denied to be a dangerous one? Dangerous it unquestionably is, to every government which has for its actual end or object, the greatest happiness of a certain one, with or without the addition of some comparatively small number of others...

Jeremy Bentham, An Introduction to the Principles of Morals and Legislation, 1789

(A) Provide TWO pieces of evidence that support Bentham's position and explain how they support the position.

(B) Provide ONE piece of evidence that undermines Bentham's position and explain how it undermines the position.

11. Use the excerpt and the image as well as your knowledge of European history to answer all parts of the question that follows.

"My Lord, in the case of Taylor, Ibbotson & Co. I took the evidence from the mouths of the boys themselves. They stated to me that they commenced working on Friday morning, the 27th of May last, at six A.M., and that, with the exception of meal hours and one hour at midnight extra, they did not cease working till four o'clock on Saturday evening, having been two days and a night thus engaged. Believing the case scarcely possible, I asked every boy the same questions, and from each received the same answers. I then went into the house to look at the time book, and in the presence of one of the masters, referred to the cruelty of the case, and stated that I should certainly punish it with all the severity in my power. Mr Rayner, the certificating surgeon of Bastile, was with me at the time."

Extract from a Factory Inspectors report,
British Parliamentary Papers No. 353, 1836

Photograph of workers in a factory, 1903

(A) Briefly identify and describe ONE cause of the situation described and pictured above.

(B) Briefly identify and describe ONE result of the situation described and pictured above.

(C) Briefly identify and describe a similar situation in ONE country other than England.

12. Answer all parts of the question.

Historians have suggested that, as the industrial revolution expanded from Great Britain to the continent, the state played a larger role in the process.

(A) Identify TWO pieces of evidence that support this argument and explain how each supports the argument.

(B) Identify ONE piece of evidence that undermines this argument and explain how the evidence undermines the argument.

Section 4: 1914–Present

13. Use the excerpt and your knowledge of European history to answer all parts of the question that follows.

…The principles to be applied are these:

First, that each part of the final settlement must be based upon the essential justice of that particular case and upon such adjustments as are most likely to bring a peace that will be permanent;

Second, that peoples and provinces are not to be bartered about from sovereignty to sovereignty as if they were mere chattels and pawns in a game, even the great game, now forever discredited, of the balance of power; but that

Third, every territorial settlement involved in this war must be made in the interest and for the benefit of the populations concerned, and not as a part of any mere adjustment or compromise of claims amongst rival states.

President Wilson, Addendum to the Fourteen
Points, February 11, 1918

(A) Briefly identify and describe ONE cause of Wilson's statement.

(B) Briefly identify and describe TWO results of Wilson's statement.

14. Use the excerpt and your knowledge of European history to answer all parts of the question that follows.

One factor in Thatcher's electoral victory had been her commitment to a reduction of immigration. In a population of 53 million whites, Britain had 1 million people of West Indian origin and an equal number of Asians. Conservatives claimed that British civilization was threatened; workers feared competition from the immigrants; and some immigrant communities had a high incidence of crime, family breakdown, illegitimacy, and disorder. An English nationalist to the core, Thatcher shared the uneasiness of many of her countrymen about pockets of poorly assimilated immigrants. The challenge was to prepare legislation that was undeniably racist without appearing to be racist.

The solution adopted was a new definition of British citizenship that sloughed off the long-standing claims of Commonwealth residents. The Nationality Act of 1981 defined British citizenship as something other than being a subject of the queen. Full British citizenship went to people who resided in Britain or were closely related to citizens. The eligibility of Commonwealth immigrants for citizenship was restricted to people who had one parent or grandparent born in the United Kingdom.

The Nationality Bill had considerable support in both parties: the

Conservatives were strong nationalists, and Labour wanted to protect jobs and keep wages up. The bill was strongly opposed by immigrant groups and the churches. It faced opposition in the House of Lords, where the Archbishop of Canterbury was a prominent opponent. Passage of the Nationality Act terminated the right of millions of former imperial subjects to settle in Britain. Essentially, the question of Commonwealth immigration was settled. Thatcher had fulfilled her campaign promise.

Earl A. Reitan, The Thatcher Revolution: Margaret Thatcher, John Major, Tony Blair, and the Transformation of Modern Britain, *2002*

(A) Provide ONE piece of evidence that supports Reitan's position that the Nationality Bill of 1981 was essentially racist.

(B) Provide ONE piece of evidence that undermines Reitan's position that the Nationality Bill of 1981 was essentially racist.

(C) Identify ONE country other than Britain that took similar actions in response to immigration.

15. Answer all parts of the question.

Historians argue whether the artistic movements of the interwar period from 1919–1939 were new reactions to the brutality of World War I or extensions of trends begun before the war.

(A) Identify TWO pieces of evidence that support the argument that interwar artistic movements were reactions to the First World War.

(B) Identify ONE piece of evidence that supports the argument that interwar artistic movements were extensions of prewar trends in art.

16. Use the excerpt and your knowledge of European history to answer all parts of the question that follows.

Unlike the purges of 1933, during which opponents of collectivization and Ukrainizers had been purged, in 1937 Stalin decided to liquidate the entire leadership of the Ukrainian Soviet government and the CPU ... By June 1938 the top seventeen ministers of the Ukrainian Soviet government were arrested and executed. The prime minister, Liubchenko, committed suicide. Almost the entire Central Committee and Politburo of Ukraine perished. An estimated 37% of the Communist party members in Ukraine - about 170,000 people - were purged. In the words of Nikita Khrushchev, Moscow's new viceroy in Kiev, the Ukrainian party "had been purged spotless." The NKVD slated for extermination entire categories of people, such as kulaks, priests, former members of anti-Bolshevik armies, those who had been abroad or had relatives abroad, and immigrants from Galicia; even average citizens perished in huge numbers. An indication of the vast scope of the Great Purge was the discovery, during the Second World War, in Vinnytsia, of a mass grave containing 10,000 bodies of residents of the region who were shot between 1937 and 1938.

Orest Subtelny, **Ukraine: A History,** *1993*

(A) Briefly identify and describe ONE cause of the events described above.

(B) Briefly identify and describe ONE result of the events described above.

(C) Briefly identify and describe similar actions taken by ONE country other than Russia.

Part 2
Practice Tests

About the Practice Tests

E ach of the following practice tests has been designed to simulate the essay section on an actual Advanced Placement European History exam. Just like on test day, you will have a total of 90 minutes to complete each practice test—15 minutes reading time and 75 minutes writing time. Although it is suggested that students use 45 minutes to write the DBQ and 30 minutes for the LEQ, the only requirement is the 15-minute reading period. Test-takers will receive only the questions—no essay booklets—until the end of the required reading period.

Complete each practice test in its entirety, then score your responses using the rubric guides in Part 1 of the Instructional Handbook before continuing on to the next practice test. If you have thoroughly reviewed each topic and practice exercise in this book, you should expect to score 6 or 7 on each of your essays.

Practice Test 1

Section A—DBQ

Directions: For the following question, use 15 minutes to analyze the documents and outline your response. At the end of this prewriting period, you will have 45 minutes to write your response.

Question 1: Analyze the methods employed by Ferdinand and Isabella to unify Spain.

Document A

SOURCE: **Anonymous Castilian noble, writing of Enrique IV, 1464**

Instead of pursuing a war against the Moors, he wars on his own vassals, on good manners, and on ancient laws.

Document B

SOURCE: **Isabella of Castile, letter to Enrique IV, 1468**

I consulted with the grandees, prelates and cabelleros about the matter. They responded that marrying the king of Portugal in no manner redounded to the benefit of your kingdoms ... but all praised and approved the marriage with the Prince of Aragon, King of Sicily.

Document C

> **SOURCE: Tomás de Torquemada, Dominican confessor of Isabella, 1472**
>
> If you ever come to the throne, you must devote yourself to the liquidation of heresy, for the glory of God and the exaltation of the Catholic Church.

Document D

> **SOURCE: Motto of Ferdinand and Isabella**
>
> Tanto monta, monta tanto—Isabel como Fernando (As much as the one is worth so much is the other worth—Isabella as Ferdinand)

Document E

> **SOURCE: Queen Isabella, on a tour through the Extremadura (a rebellious territory), 1477**
>
> I have come to this land, and I do not intend to leave it, not to flee danger nor to shirk my duty. Nor will I give comfort to my enemies who cause such pain to my subjects.

Document F

> **SOURCE: Spanish chronicler, upon the birth of a male heir to Ferdinand and Isabella, 1478**
>
> Clearly we see ourselves given a very special gift by God, for at the end of such a long wait, He has desired to give him to us. The queen has paid to this kingdom the debt of virile succession that she is obligated to do. It is clear that this queen is moved to do things by divine Inspiration. ... God has chosen the tribe of Isabella which he prefers.

Document G

> SOURCE: **Andres Bernaldez, Curate of the Palace (official court chronicler), 1480**
>
> This accursed race [the Conversos] is either unwilling to bring their children to be baptized, or if they do, they wash away the stain on returning home. … With many other abominable ceremonies of their religion, they entertain no respect for monastic life, and frequently profane the sanctity of religious houses in violation or seduction of their names.

Document H

> SOURCE: **Niccolo Machiavelli, *The Prince*, writing about Ferdinand, 1505**
>
> At the beginning of his reign he attacked Granada. …he kept the minds of the barons of Castile occupied with this undertaking…. By this means he acquired prestige and power over them without their becoming aware of it…

Section B—LEQ

Directions: Choose ONE of the following questions and write a response that meets all the requirements of the LEQ rubric. You should complete your response within 30 minutes.

Question 2: *Compare and contrast the motives of the participants in the French Wars of Religion with those of the participants in the Thirty Years War?*

Question 3: *Compare and contrast the power of the middle class in eighteenth-century England and France.*

Practice Test 2

Section A—DBQ

Directions: For the following question, use 15 minutes to analyze the documents and outline your response. At the end of this prewriting period, you will have 45 minutes to write your response.

Question 1: *Analyze the factors that contributed to the Ottoman defeat of Rhodes.*

Document A

SOURCE: **Anonymous Ottoman chronicler, writing of the slave traders on Rhodes, circa 1300**

How many sons of the Prophet are captured by these children of lies? … How many thousands of the faithful are forced to turn infidel? How many wives and children? Their wickedness knows no end.

Document B

SOURCE: **Pope Pius II, in defense of the Knights of St. John (Hospitallers), circa 1450**

…if all the other Christian princes … had shown themselves as tireless in their hostility to the Turks as the single island of Rhodes had done, that impious people would not have grown so strong.

Document C

SOURCE: Pope Leo X, upon the Ottoman capture of Egypt, 1517

Now that the Terrible Turk has Egypt and Alexandria and the whole of the Roman eastern empire in his power and has equipped a massive fleet in the Dardanelles, he will swallow not just Sicily and Italy but the whole world.

Document D

SOURCE: Bartolomeo Contarini, Venetian businessman, 1520

Rumour has it that Suleiman is aptly named ... is knowledgeable and shows good judgement.

Document E

SOURCE: Suleiman, Sultan of the Ottoman Empire, letter to Philip de L'Isle Adam, 10 September 1521

Suleiman the sultan, by the grace of God, king of kings, sovereign of sovereigns, most high emperor of Byzantium and Trebizond, very powerful king of Persia, of Arabia, of Syria, and of Egypt, supreme lord of Europe, and of Asia, prince of Mecca and Aleppo, lord of Jerusalem, and ruler of the universal sea, to Philip de L'Isle Adam, Grand Master of the island of Rhodes, greetings.

I congratulate you upon your new dignity, and upon your arrival within your territories. I trust that you will rule there prosperously, and with even more glory than your predecessors. I also mean to cultivate your favour. Rejoice then with me, as a very dear friend, that following in the footsteps of my father, who conquered Persia, Jerusalem, Arabia and Egypt, I have captured that most powerful of fortresses, Belgrade, during the late Autumn. After which, having offered battle to the Infidel, which they had not courage to accept, I took many other beautiful and well-fortified cities, and destroyed most of their inhabitants either by sword or fire, the remainder being reduced to slavery. Now after sending my numerous and victorious army into their winter quarters, I shall myself return in triumph to my court at Constantinople.

Document F

> **SOURCE: Philippe de L'Isle, letter to the king of France, 19 September 1521**
>
> Sire, since he became Grand Turk, this is the first letter that he has sent to Rhodes, and we do not accept it as a token of friendship, but rather as a veiled threat.

Document G

> **SOURCE: Suleiman, Sultan of the Ottoman Empire, letter to Philip de L'Isle, 10 June 1522**
>
> The Sultan Suleiman to Villiers de L'Isle Adam, Grand Master of Rhodes, to his Knights, and to the people at large. Your monstrous injuries against my most afflicted people have aroused my pity and indignation. I command you, therefore, instantly to surrender the island and fortress of Rhodes, and I give you my gracious permission to depart in safety with the most precious of your effects; or if you desire to remain under my government, I shall not require of you any tribute, or do anything in diminution of your liberties, or against your religion. If you are wise, you will prefer friendship and peace to cruel war…

Document H

> **SOURCE: Suleiman, to his vizier regarding L'Isle Adam, 24 December 1522**
>
> It saddens me to be compelled to cast this brave old man out of his home.

Section B—LEQ

Directions: Choose ONE of the following questions and write a response that meets all the requirements of the LEQ rubric. You should complete your response within 30 minutes.

Question 2: In what ways did socialist policy influence the roles of women in post-WWII Europe?

Question 3: In what ways did Napoleonic rule influence the roles of women in post-revolutionary France?

3

Practice Test 3

Section A—DBQ

Directions: For the following question, use 15 minutes to analyze the documents and outline your response. At the end of this prewriting period, you will have 45 minutes to write your response.

> **Question 1:** *Analyze the conditions of and responses to women in the workplace in Europe in the 19th and early 20th centuries.*

Document A

SOURCE: from "What Are Women Doing?", English Woman's Journal, March 1861

If choice of occupation is what you want, surely it may be said, here it is in abundance. But there is one notable fact which ought not to be overlooked: namely, that whatever mill, yard, factory or workshop you enter, you will find the women in the lowest, the dirtiest, and the unhealthiest departments. The reason is simple. The manager of a business naturally asks who will do the inferior work at the lowest rate, and as women's labor is the cheapest, it falls as a matter of course to their share. It is an undeniable fact that in this country a very large proportion of the hard labor is done by women.

Document B

> **SOURCE: Jenny Heynrichs, in "What is Work?", Germany, 1866**
>
> Who could deny that the vocation of wife and mother is the highest, most sacred and most fulfilling that can fall to the lot of women. Who could deny that the work involved in this calling makes her a most praiseworthy and useful member of society. But who could fail to perceive that, given our established social conditions and the way they have come about through progressive development, a great many young women remain unmarried, unprovided for and dissatisfied.

Document C

> **SOURCE: Gertrude J. King, secretary, from a form letter to English businessmen, 1877**
>
> Women as a rule are quick workers; the salaries paid to them when thoroughly trained to office work, average from 20/- to 30/- weekly; and, a sedentary occupation being suitable to them, they can perfectly well work for long hours when necessary. The employment of men and women in the same establishment is found to improve the moral tone of both; mutual respect is engendered and the work does not suffer. This is the actual experience of many shops, and of offices, both under government and otherwise.
>
> It is necessary to point out here the advantages which would accrue to the community if more of our surplus women became breadwinners instead of mere consumers, and I would ask you to help our efforts to obtain for women clerks work, which they are quite capable of performing, whenever an opening may occur in your own office or elsewhere.

Document D

> **Source: A brief on opening the German civil service to women, Germany, 1878**
>
> Every male employee automatically has the right to a two-week summer vacation. Not so the ladies. If a lady takes a leave of absence on the basis of a medical certificate, she is obliged to pay her substitute the daily remuneration, arbitrarily fixed at a high rate.

Document E

> **Source: Amalie Seidl, "Women Workers Strike," Austria, 1893**
>
> About twenty years ago, conditions in the Viennese textile industry were considerably worse than they are now, which doesn't mean that women workers today have cause for satisfaction. In 1892, when at the age of 16 I began working in a textile factory, the work day was from 6 in the morning to 7 in the evening. The workers were not organized and had to be satisfied with wages of Kronen 1 to Kr. 1.50 a day. One cannot imagine how low the living standard was for women workers.

Document F

> **Source: "Charter of Reforms," Women's Co-operative Guild, England, 1897**
>
> One of the great evils that shop assistants suffer from in ordinary shops, especially where they "live in," is the short time allowed for meals and rest. We hear of half-an-hour for dinner and a quarter-of-an-hour for tea being the whole time in a day of thirteen or fourteen hours, which a girl has, not only for meals, but for rest also. And even this time is often shortened if customers happen to come in at meal times. In the report of the labor commissioners, evidence is given showing how bad this is for the girls, who have not time to eat a proper meal in the middle of the day, and are too worn-out to eat it at night; whose health is injured by "bolting" their food, and who suffer from illnesses brought on by the long hours of standing. / Guild members who deal only at their stores can feel satisfied that the girls who serve them are not suffering in this way.

Document G

> **SOURCE: from "A Shop Girl's Day in a Clothing Store," *The Wife of the Future*, France, December 1897**
>
> In the clothing business there are two seasons very different from one another: one is the heavy season and the other the slow. / The heavy season causes terrible fatigue as you can judge from this account. / Arriving at 8:15 in the morning, going down the racks, repeated trips to the stockroom to bring down the merchandise which is likely to be sold during the day (about two thousand garments are sold in a day). / The storeroom is on the sixth floor and the saleswomen carry the clothes down on their arms or balance them against their hips.

Document H

> **SOURCE: Paula Mueller, from the curriculum for a school established to train women to become social workers, Germany, 1905**
>
> There is an increasing urgency for women to contribute to the solution of the problems of our times. Women have come to recognize the practice of social work as their right. But in order to be able to fulfill this duty and to carry out such a responsibility, one needs training.

Section B—LEQ

Directions: Choose ONE of the following questions and write a response that meets all the requirements of the LEQ rubric. You should complete your response within 30 minutes.

Question 2: *Compare and contrast the art of the Renaissance with that of the Baroque period.*

Question 3: *Compare and contrast the art of the Enlightenment in the 18th century with that of the interwar period in the 20th century.*

Part 3

Answers & Explanations

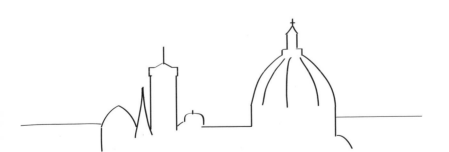

Step

2 (LEQ)

Brainstorming and Organizing Evidence

1. ORIGINS OF CHRISTIAN HUMANISM

Exercise Question: Assess the extent to which Christian Humanism traced its roots to Italian Humanists.

Italian Humanists	Petrarch	- Studied classics - Virtue and truth are the highest goals
	Boccaccio	- The Decameron
	Poggio	- Saved and translated many classics at Constance
	Lorenzo Valla	- Debunked some historical claims of Church (Donation of Constantine)
	Giannozzo Manetti	- Greek & Latin scholar
	Leonardo Bruni	- Wrote History of Florence
	Marsilio Ficino	- Platonic scholar
	Cristoforo Landino	- Humanist teacher
	Medici, Visconti, Sforza, Gonzaga, Este families	- Actively supported humanism in their domains

Italian Humanists (cont'd)	Nicholas V	- Supported the collection of classical manuscripts
	Sixtus IV	- Re-established Vatican Library
	Leo X	- Supported humanist works
	Niccolo Machiavelli	- Political humanist
Christian Humanists	Erasmus of Rotterdam	- Classical scholar and theologian (pupil of Colet); - Satirized Church abuses
	Thomas More	- *Utopia*—humanist social critique
	John Colet	- Applied humanist technique to study of the Bible

Christian Humanists in this list mimic some of the practices of their Italian counterparts. For instance, More's *Utopia* is an obvious imitation of a technique used by the ancient Greeks to critique society—literary utopianism. Plato's *Republic* is one example of classical utopian literature that was studied with great enthusiasm by Italian Humanists. Erasmus and Colet both used humanist techniques to study the Bible, but both clearly leaned away from the more secular subjects of the Italian Humanists.

Example categories of evidence that might be used to answer this question:

Shared Humanist Techniques

- Petrarch – studied classical works
- More – *Utopia* (based on classical models)
- Colet – used Humanist techniques to study the Bible

Italian Humanist Subjects

- Boccaccio – *Decameron* focuses on life during the Black Death in Florence
- Bruni – wrote a history of Florence
- Machiavelli – focused on history and politics

Christian Humanist Subjects

- Erasmus – focused on Church and Christian theology
- Colet – studied the Bible

2. THE ROMAN CATHOLIC CHURCH AND ASTRONOMY

Exercise Question: Analyze the impact of Roman Catholic doctrine on the study of astronomy in the 16th and 17th centuries.

Astronomy	Influences
Geocentrism	- Supported by Ptolemy and Aristotle - Aligned with Church doctrine of Man at the center
Copernicus	- Charted stars for the Church - Observations led him to Heliocentric Theory - Devotion to Church led him to publish posthumously
Galileo	- Observations led him to support Copernican ideas - Inquisition forced him to recant

The Church was influenced by Aristotelian and Scholastic thought, both of which supported a geocentric universe and a reliance on the ideas of past thinkers, rather than observation and reason. The Church in the 16th century was also influenced by pressures exerted on it in the Protestant Reformation. All of these influences led the Church to oppose the ideas of Galileo and to attempt to suppress those ideas through the Inquisition and Index. Ironically, Galileo's ideas were influenced by Copernicus, a churchman who charted the stars and planets as part of his duties within the Church. Copernicus realized through his work that the geocentric universe was flawed and created a written work to defend the theory of heliocentrism. Because of the influence of the Catholic Church, Copernicus chose to delay publication of his work until after his death.

Example categories of evidence that might be used to answer this question:

Church supported Aristotelian ideas that aligned with Church doctrine

- Ptolemy

- Aristotle

- Geocentrism

Church provided education that promoted scientific observation

- Copernicus

- Star mapping

- Revolutions of the Heavenly Bodies

Church used its power to silence opposition views

- Galileo

- Inquisition

- Index

3. ENLIGHTENMENT OPTIMISM

Exercise Question: To what extent were the ideas of the
Enlightenment expressions of optimism about humanity?

Enlightenment Ideas	Underlying Assumptions about People
Popular sovereignty	- People are capable of self-government (Locke) - Popular sovereignty will be good for all (Locke) - People are generally good-willed (Locke, Rousseau) - Rule by the people is better than monarchy (Rousseau)
Faith in human reason	- People can solve problems through reason (Descartes, Bayle, Diderot)
Deism	- God is not needed after creation (English Empiricists, d'Holbach) - God is satisfied that man could be trusted (Voltaire) - People do not need organized religion (Voltaire, Bayle)
Social contract	- People must sacrifice some liberty to enjoy government protection (Hobbes, Locke) - Governments must exist to protect people from each other (Hobbes)

In what ways is it TRUE? People are generally good and
trustworthy (popular sovereignty, deism, reason). People are capable
(popular sovereignty, reason, deism).

In what ways is it FALSE? Individuals may be bad leaders (popular sovereignty, social contract). Those in power may not always protect the interests of the group (popular sovereignty, deism, social contract, social justice).

Example categories of evidence that might be used to answer this question:

People are generally good and trustworthy

- Popular sovereignty
- Deism
- Reason
- Locke
- Rousseau

People are capable

- Popular sovereignty
- Deism
- Reason
- Locke
- d'Holbach
- Voltaire

Leaders may be corrupt and fail to protect the interests of the group

- Popular sovereignty
- Social contract
- Social justice
- Locke
- Rousseau
- Hobbes

4. CONGRESS OF VIENNA

Exercise Question: *Analyze the ways in which the Congress of Vienna used conservative political theory to create stability in post-Napoleonic Europe.*

- "Citoyens" and "Citoyennes"

- Juring Clergy

- Civil Constitution of the Clergy

- Regicide

- Louis XVI

- Marie Antoinette

- The Terror

- Robespierre

- Guillotine

- Committee of Public Safety

- War with Austria

- Robespierre

- Danton

- Status quo

- Social stratification

- Hobbes

Example categories of evidence that might be used to answer this question:

Congress pointed to Liberal excesses and other "evils" of French Revolution

- Equality across class divisions ("Citoyens" and "Citoyennes")

- Rejection of Roman Catholic dogma (Juring Clergy, Civil Constitution of the Clergy)

- Regicide (Louis XVI, Marie Antoinette)

- The Terror (Robespierre, guillotine, Committee of Public Safety)

- Internationalized revolution (War with Austria)

Congress stereotyped Liberals as Extremists

- Robespierre
- Danton

Congress used Conservative principles to restore order in Europe

- Status quo
- Social stratification
- Monarchical rule (Hobbes)

5. UNIFICATION OF ITALY AND GERMANY

Exercise Question: Compare and contrast the influence of nationalism on Italian and German unification.

Italian Nationalism

- Mazzini
- Garibaldi
- Red Shirts
- Naples
- Young Italy
- liberal

Italian Officials

- Cavour
- Victor Emmanuel

German Nationalism

- Herder
- Fichte
- Volk
- militarist
- conservative

German Officials

- Bismarck
- Wilhelm I
- Prussia

Example categories of evidence that might be used to answer this question:

Both used nationalism for unification

- Garibaldi
- Mazzini
- Young Italians
- Volk
- Herder
- Fichte

Germans controlled national spirit

- Militarist
- Bismarck
- Wilhelm I
- Prussia

Italians struggled to control nationalism

- Garibaldi
- Red Shirts
- Naples
- Cavour
- Victor Emmanuel

6. INTERWAR ART

Exercise Question: *To what extent was Interwar Art unique from art of pre-World War I?*

Irrationalism

- Friedrich Nietzsche
- Fyodor Dostoevsky
- Henri Bergson
- Georges Sorel
- Dante Gabriel Rossetti
- Oscar Wilde
- Dadaism

Surrealism

- Salvador Dali
- Max Ernst
- Pablo Picasso

Postwar Artistic Technique

- Use of color based in earlier palettes (Franz Marc)
- Postwar artists were students of prior artists
- Some postwar artists worked through war (Modigliani)

Example categories of evidence that might be used to answer this question:

Postwar artists imitated colors and styles of earlier artists (not unique)

- Franz Marc
- Picasso
- Surrealism
- Friedrich Nietzsche
- Fyodor Dostoevsky

Postwar artists included some whose work predates the war (not unique)

- Modigliani
- Picasso
- Ernst

Surrealist art was, at least partially, reaction to the war (unique)

- Dali
- Ernst
- Picasso

7. WWII CONFERENCES AND COLD WAR POLICY

Exercise Question: Analyze the impact of WWII Allied conferences on subsequent Cold War policy.

Allied Conferences

- Washington (Churchill, FDR)
- Casablanca (Churchill, FDR, de Gaulle)
- Cairo (Churchill, FDR, Chiang Kai-shek)
- Teheran (Churchill, FDR, Stalin)
- San Francisco (UN)
- Malta (Churchill, FDR)
- Yalta (Churchill, FDR, Stalin)
- Potsdam (Churchill, Attlee, Truman, Stalin)

Major Players

- Churchill
- FDR
- Stalin
- Truman
- Chiang Kai-shek

Cold War Policies/ Organizations

- NATO
- SEATO
- Warsaw Pact
- Buffer states
- Berlin Wall
- Mutually Assured Destruction
- United Nations

Example categories of evidence that might be used to answer this question:

Exclusion of Soviets from early Allied conferences

- Washington
- Casablanca
- Cairo

Animosity between Stalin and Churchill

- Stalin
- Churchill

American diplomacy isolated Soviets

- San Francisco
- UN
- NATO
- SEATO

8. ANTI-SOVIET UPRISINGS IN EASTERN EUROPE

Exercise Question: *Discuss the reasons for the successes and failures of anti-Soviet uprisings in Eastern Europe 1950–1989.*

Rebellions	Brezhnev Doctrine
- Czechoslovakia (Prague Spring)	- Yugoslavia
- East Germany	- Perestroika
- Hungary	- Glasnost
- Poland	- SALT
- Soviet Policy	

Key Players
- Stalin
- Khrushchev
- Brezhnev
- Gorbachev
- Tito
- Nagy
- Jaruzelski (Solidarity)

Example categories of evidence that might be used to answer this question:

Nuclear threat prevented Western assistance (pre-1970 failures)

- Khrushchev
- Brezhnev
- Czechoslovakia
- Hungary

Suppression of Soviet dissent (pre-1970 failures)

- Brezhnev Doctrine
- Khrushchev
- Brezhnev
- Czechoslovakia
- Hungary

Glasnost and reduced nuclear threat (post-1970 successes)

- Gorbachev
- SALT
- Brezhnev
- Glasnost
- Perestroika
- Poland

Step 2 (DBQ)

Using the 3-Step Process to Analyze Documents for the DBQ

1. FRENCH WARS OF RELIGION

Document A

SUMMARIZE – Jeanne d'Albret says that Margaret's religious beliefs will make the difference between a marriage that is good for France and one that is the ruin of the Bourbon family. She implies that Margaret is well known for her support of the Roman Catholic church.

ANALYZE – The document seems to place religion at the center of the debate, but it could also be used to support underlying political causes because it connects religion to the success or failure of the House of Bourbon.

CRITICIZE – It would seem that, since her power increases with the proposed marriage, d'Albret might express a genuine concern in a letter to her son.

Document B

SUMMARIZE – Charles IX says that he favors the marriage even if the Pope opposes it.

ANALYZE – This could be used to support the contention that politics outweighs religion in diplomacy.

CRITICIZE – Without further evidence about the king's possible motives, it is possible that he is being forthright with his aunt. Additionally, the traditional politico-religious struggle between the French monarchy and the Roman papacy could lend credence to the attitude expressed in the document.

Document C

SUMMARIZE – Salviati writes that his account of the killing of Admiral

Coligny is accurate, and that the regent, Anjou, Nemours, and Guise were those responsible for the shooting as well as the killing of "the others." He also says that the king was unaware of the plot.

ANALYZE – This might be used to corroborate the political motives expressed by others who were closer to the events.

CRITICIZE – Salviati's dispatch is likely one of a series of letters to the Vatican describing events in France. Since it is his job to chronicle these events, it is likely that these details are accurate to the best of his knowledge. Additionally (and perhaps more importantly), for Salviati to attack the French Catholics in a battle with the Huguenots, he likely felt more certain of his facts.

Document D

SUMMARIZE – Henry of Valois says that he and the regent were convinced that the king was in danger because of the fighting between the Huguenots and the Catholics, and that Coligny had led the king to believe that Valois and the regent were working against the king. The latter explained why he wanted Coligny dead and the former reason was provided to the king to justify the killing.

ANALYZE – This might help to support the politics behind the wars.

CRITICIZE – Again, the source cites a "conversation," so the motives of the recorder should be considered. It is possible that Henry is attempting to justify his involvement in the massacre as he looks back on it.

Document E

SUMMARIZE – Busbecq describes the effects of the wars as horrible. He also says that beyond religious differences, there are disputes among the leading families, presumably political disputes.

ANALYZE – This easily supports politics as an underlying cause of the wars.

CRITICIZE – Busbecq seems to be an outside (and therefore possibly objective) observer, so his assessment of the situation could be more reliable than those of the insiders.

Document F

SUMMARIZE – The edict states clearly that Catholics and Huguenots are both free to practice their religions in France. It also says that anything that either side did to the other during the wars is "forgotten."

ANALYZE – This seems to support the religious causes of the wars.

CRITICIZE – Since you might be expected to know some of the details surrounding the Edict of Nantes, one could say that Henry's declaration of "religious tolerance" was necessary to calm the political winds surrounding his ascension to the throne.

Document G

SUMMARIZE – The painting shows all manner of inhumanity committed as part of the attack on the Huguenots.

ANALYZE – Besides supporting the brutality of the wars, the official-looking soldiers might support political causes.

CRITICIZE – Unless you know that Dubois was a Huguenot painter, POV might be difficult with this document. If the painter's origins are understood, then it could be said that he may have depicted the Catholics more harshly than they deserved because of his relation to those massacred.

Outside Evidence:

- Henry of Navarre (Henry IV) sacrifices his religious beliefs for the sake of securing the throne

Possible Categories of Evidence:

- Concerns for success of Bourbon family: A, Henry IV

- Underlying political causes: B, C, D, E, G

- Religion drives politics: A, B, F, G

2.   17ᴛʜ-CENTURY SWEDISH EMPIRE

Document A

SUMMARIZE – The document transcribes a conversation in which the future king of Sweden explains to his tutor that he would rather be bold and dead than careful and alive.

ANALYZE – It might be used as evidence of the character of Charles XII.

CRITICIZE – Like other transcriptions, the recorder may have specific motives for writing this document. Since we don't know who transcribed this conversation, POV is difficult for this document.

Document B

SUMMARIZE – Charles XI explains that his son's education should be based on humility, Christian values, and other qualities necessary to prepare him to be a good king.

ANALYZE – This can be used to support a statement about the character of Charles XI.

CRITICIZE – Since Charles XI is king and he probably knew these proscriptions would be read (or related) widely, he may have set down his educational/moral objectives as a model for all, as much as a general guide for his son's tutor.

Document C

SUMMARIZE – This declaration affirms the absolute power of Charles XI.

ANALYZE – The document might serve to support the king's responsibility in the successes or failures of the kingdom.

CRITICIZE – Since this declaration was issued before Charles XII took the throne, it might be that his father was attempting to prepare the way for his son's accession. Because Charles XI would have known that everyone would have access to this document, it is likely that the strong tone of the declaration was meant to impress, if not intimidate, his son's future subjects.

Document D

SUMMARIZE – The French ambassador describes a change in the tone of the court since Charles XII assumed the throne.

ANALYZE – Along with docs A and B, this document might be used to demonstrate the differences in ruling styles of Charles XI and his son.

CRITICIZE – Although the audience is unknown and the intent is unclear, as a French ambassador, D'Avaux can be described as an outsider to Sweden, so he might see, even more clearly than the Swedes, the differences between the courts of Charles XI and his son.

Document E

SUMMARIZE – Charles XII explains his intentions in a future war.

ANALYZE – The evidence might be helpful in assessing decisions of the king.

CRITICIZE – The tone of bravado expressed in this document might help to argue the king's bold (if not cavalier) attitude.

Document F

SUMMARIZE – A Swedish officer seems to be criticizing the war effort.

ANALYZE – This is another document addressing the king's decisions.

CRITICIZE – It is likely that this officer never intended this statement to be read publically, so it may be excerpted from a private letter or journal, and this could be Cederhjelm's true opinion of the war effort.

Document G

SUMMARIZE – Charles XII explains why he refuses to settle the war.

ANALYZE – This document can be used to support statements about the king's character as well as his decisions.

CRITICIZE – Charles's tone is one of condemnation. Although he may not have intended to for the letter to be read outside his minister's office, it is likely that Charles knew that any official letter could be scrutinized later. This fact makes his overt criticism that much more scathing.

Outside Evidence:

- Battle of Narva (Swedish success over Russia)

- Peter the Great

- Russian naval power

Possible Categories of Evidence:

- Charles XII's rashness: A, C, E

- Charles XII's stubbornness: C, G, Narva, Peter's navy

- King's noble intentions: B, E

- King's ability to lead: D, F

- King's openness to advice: C, D

3. THE DISAPPEARANCE OF POLAND

Document A

SUMMARIZE – Niemirycz says that the greatest aspect of Polish society is liberty.

ANALYZE – The document may be useful in analyzing forces within Poland.

CRITICIZE – Since this is from a speech, it might be that Niemirycz's words are meant to inspire or convince his audience. The concept of "liberty" may be a rhetorical tool.

Document B

SUMMARIZE – Williams suggests that Poland's liberty is actually a bad thing.

ANALYZE – The document might help to characterize the forces outside of Poland, as well as those within the country as seen through an outsider's eyes.

CRITICIZE – Williams might envision England's government as the best available—a view not uncommon inside and outside of Britain in the 18th century. By comparison, liberty (an Enlightenment notion not yet tested in real life) may indeed seem "noxious."

Document C

SUMMARIZE – Soltyck says that he will not sign the partition agreement.

ANALYZE – This is another document that contrasts inner and outer forces and their perspectives on partition.

CRITICIZE – Since this is Soltyck's resignation letter, it is likely that, although he may be unhappy with the partition, he has overstated his position somewhat for effect. If Poland is partitioned, he has nothing to lose because he is likely out of power anyway.

Document D

SUMMARIZE – Rejtan says that he also opposes partition.

ANALYZE – The document further supports the view that forces inside Poland opposed partition.

CRITICIZE – The emphatic tone of this and the previous document help to argue the importance of the partition issue within Poland, particularly the level of opposition.

Document E

SUMMARIZE – Mirabeau expresses an opinion about the partition and its causes.

ANALYZE – This evidence supports the influence of outside forces in the partition.

CRITICIZE – Even without an understanding of Mirabeau's ideals, the use of the word "whims" implies that he sees despotism as capricious. His opposition to the partition may be based more on these opinions than on his views of Polish society.

Document F

SUMMARIZE – Marx praises the constitution as a uniquely generous act by a privileged class.

ANALYZE – The document is evidence of an outsider's view of actions within Poland.

CRITICIZE – Marx is describing events in Poland as part of his history of Europe, in which he sees all monarchies as oppressors. A constitution that would expel the foreigners and allow for self-rule would naturally appeal to him. Additionally, since Marx is not writing for at least 40–50 years after the constitution, he has the benefit of hindsight in choosing his words.

Document G

SUMMARIZE – Kosciuszko declares his intentions in the insurrection of Cracow against the forces for partition.

ANALYZE – The document might be used to support an argument faulting outside forces for the partition. It could also serve to support an argument that forces within Poland opposed partition.

CRITICIZE – It is likely that any insurrection, if unsuccessful, will be harshly punished, so Kosciuszko has nothing to lose by publicly declaring his intentions. Only if this declaration can inspire other Poles, will he have a chance at success.

Document H

SUMMARIZE – Gardner describes the actions of those enforcing the partition.

ANALYZE – The document might be used to characterize the outside forces as well as the partition itself.

CRITICIZE – Given the opinions of other British observers in previous documents, it may be that Gardner, too, expected the partition to be best for all involved. That sort of expectation could lead him to great disappointment about the actual nature of the partition.

Outside Evidence:

- Catherine the Great

Possible Categories of Evidence:

- "Liberty": A, B, C, D

- Polish cooperation: C, D

- "Best" for Poland: B, F

- Self-serving foreigners: E, Catherine the Great

4. NAPOLEON IN EGYPT

Document A

SUMMARIZE – al-Jabarti describes the good times in Egyptian society before Napoleon.

ANALYZE – The evidence may support an argument that Napoleon's impact on society was negative.

CRITICIZE – As an Egyptian, al-Jabarti may be influenced by a sense of national pride and, consequently, he may be expected to view Napoleon's conquest as a negative event in Egyptian history.

Document B

SUMMARIZE – Napoleon says that he opposes the Mameluke oppressors and supports the Muslims.

ANALYZE – This document could be used to support the contention that Egyptian society was improved by Napoleon's influence, or at least to counter the argument that life was good before Napoleon.

CRITICIZE – Since Napoleon's success in Egypt would benefit from support from the local population, he could be expected to distinguish French domination from Mameluke domination. Egyptian Muslims may be more easily won over if they viewed Napoleon as a kindred spirit.

Document C

SUMMARIZE – Napoleon says that the Marmelukes have no right to control Egypt, and they have kept all that is good in the country away from the people of Egypt.

ANALYZE – Again, the document implies that Napoleon will improve the society (and perhaps the culture) for the Egyptians by eliminating the Marmelukes.

CRITICIZE – Like Document B, Napoleon may have used this public proclamation to win support from the local population.

Document D

SUMMARIZE – Bourrienne writes of Napoleon's use of public execution to secure stability in Egypt.

ANALYZE – The document says little about society or culture, but may be used to support an argument about Napoleon's methods.

CRITICIZE – It is possible that Bourrienne embellishes the situation a bit to make himself sound more humane in retrospect—30 plus years after the fact. Napoleon's ultimate fate may also give cause for Bourrienne to look more humane in his memoirs.

Document E

SUMMARIZE – Bourrienne writes that Napoleon intended to stay in Egypt to colonize it and introduce new cultural benefits.

ANALYZE – The evidence again speaks to Napoleon's motives and also serves to support the intention of cultural improvement.

CRITICIZE – Note comments for Document D. It should also be noted that any memoir written 30 years later, no matter which way the political winds blow, could be skewed by the writer's memory.

Document F

SUMMARIZE – St. John describes the effectiveness of Egyptian military training in the late 19th or early 20th century.

ANALYZE – Although the document is well outside the range of dates in this essay, it might help to support an argument that Egyptian society and culture were better after Napoleon.

CRITICIZE – If St. John is a casual observer (there is no evidence to counter that view), one could argue that his observations might be objective. One issue with this document is that it gives no indication of the date of St. John's visit, so the accuracy of his recollection might be questioned.

Document G

SUMMARIZE – Pasquier describes the impact in France of Napoleon's reports from Egypt.

ANALYZE – This document could help to legitimize Napoleon's claims to support the Muslims as stated in earlier documents.

CRITICIZE – Assuming that Pasquier wrote his memoirs after the fall of the empire, he might feel somewhat vindicated in his negative assessment of Napoleon.

Outside Evidence:

- Napoleon's rapid rise to power

- Napoleon's strategies for gaining power

Possible Categories of Evidence:

- Negative impact: A, D

- Positive impact: B, C, E, F

- Influence of French culture: C, E, F

- No attempt to impact: B, D, G, Napoleon's rise to power, Napoleon's strategies for gaining power

5. THE MIDDLE CLASS IN THE 19ᵀᴴ CENTURY

Document A

SUMMARIZE – Arnold writes that the revolts in France will inspire others outside France. He fears that, although the French rebels are intelligent, their English imitators will be insensible and brutal.

ANALYZE – The document seems to imply that the revolutions were led by "the masses."

CRITICIZE – Without any knowledge of Arnold's identity beyond "private secretary," one might say that he is likely speaking frankly about his views of the revolutions in a letter to his sister.

Document B

SUMMARIZE – Crómieux cautions against haste in establishing a new government in France to prevent the problems of the 1830 revolution.

ANALYZE – The document helps to characterize the revolution, but it says nothing specifically about the middle class.

CRITICIZE – Crómieux's position in government gives him reason to encourage calm and rationality, even if he did not support the other points in this document.

Document C

SUMMARIZE – Lamartine suggests that the revolution must consider the powerless classes.

ANALYZE – The evidence might support an argument about the participation of the masses.

CRITICIZE – With no knowledge of Lamartine's background, one might assume that he is at least interested in political self-preservation, so he is likely to believe whole-heartedly in the position he is supporting in this speech to his fellow politicians.

Document D

SUMMARIZE – Kossuth abdicates his position in favor of a military leader in order to help defend Hungary against foreign aggressors.

ANALYZE – The document says nothing of the classes, but might be helpful in supporting an argument about the motives of participants in the revolution.

CRITICIZE – The source line says nothing about Kossuth or his background, but if he is recognized as a Hungarian nationalist, it could be said that his motives for abdication are sincerely in the interest of Hungary.

Document E

SUMMARIZE – Senior writes of the belief that the middle class is the only hope for the success of the revolution.

ANALYZE – In addition to detailing the strengths of the middle class, this document might also be used to argue against the leadership of other classes.

CRITICIZE – The fact that this document comes from a journal entry of an academic might support it as a frank appraisal by an expert in the field of politics.

Document F

SUMMARIZE – Laing credits the middle class with leading the revolution in Germany because, he says, they fight for their intellectual freedom.

ANALYZE – This document may be used to support a justification of middle-class leadership.

CRITICIZE – If Laing is assumed to be an objective observer, this might also be considered a frank appraisal of the situation—this time by an outsider.

Document G

SUMMARIZE – Senior tries to explain the failure of the Italian revolution by saying that the true liberals in Italy are the middle class located in the eastern part of the country.

ANALYZE – The document might help to support the contention that without the middle class, there is no successful revolution.

CRITICIZE – The fact that this document comes from a journal entry of an academic might support it as a frank appraisal by an expert in the field of politics.

Outside Evidence:

- Louis Napoleon Bonaparte

- Louis Philippe

- Frankfurt Assembly

- Louis Kossuth

Possible Categories of Evidence:

- Middle class leads well: A, C, E, F, G, Louis Napoleon Bonaparte

- Middle class leads poorly: A, C, F, Louis Philippe, Louis Napoleon Bonaparte

- Liberals lead revolution: G, Frankfurt Assembly, Louis Kossuth

- Revolutions are bad: A, B, F

6. NATIONAL LEADERS OF THE GREAT WAR

Document A

SUMMARIZE – Wilson defines "just peace" as one that is open and fair to all nations, and he contrasts it with what has been true of past settlements.

ANALYZE – The document could be used to support Wilson's view of justice, as well as explicit evidence of one definition of just peace.

CRITICIZE – It is likely that you already know that this speech was delivered to a joint session of the US Congress, so it was meant primarily for domestic consumption. Even if you don't, it can be said that a US President in 1918, having witnessed from afar the destruction of WWI, may be inclined toward a settlement that seeks to avoid future conflicts—conflicts that inevitably involve the US. One might also say that Wilson's idealism is likely a product of his inexperience (as compared with France, Britain, and the other Allies) with the horrors wrought by the German Empire in the war.

Document B

SUMMARIZE – Thaer outlines his reasons for suing for peace.

ANALYZE – The document might help to support an argument that the Germans wanted Wilson's just peace. It might also be used to suggest that Wilson's view was at least the implied intention of the Allied powers.

CRITICIZE – It might seem obvious that the Germans would prefer Wilson's peace to the one offered by the other Allies, but in October 1918, they would have had no negotiations with the Allies, and they might not understand that Wilson's view is not universal. Additionally, most students will be familiar with the Kaiser's ambitions at the start of the war, so the Colonel's desire for peace would have had to be very strong for him to even consider this request.

Document C

SUMMARIZE – This is an excerpt from the terms of armistice.

ANALYZE – The document might be used to illustrate the outcome of armistice negotiations, and it might be used in conjunction with other evidence to develop an argument about the Allied view of justice.

CRITICIZE – Since the Germans sued for peace, the Allies may have felt they had the upper hand and no longer needed to be so "just," as defined earlier by Wilson. Even so, they may have intended this armistice to be less-than-harsh so that the Germans would not back away from the table.

Document D

SUMMARIZE – Clemenceau outlines his version of justice as penalties on those responsible for the war.

ANALYZE – This document would lend weight to an argument that defines the Allied view of justice.

CRITICIZE – Clemenceau, speaking for the French, probably needed to be mindful of his countrymen's desire for retribution. He might be politically unable to accept Wilson's view of "justice."

Document E

SUMMARIZE – Brockdorff-Rantzau implies that the Germans were deceived by the Allies. He says that the Germans expected a just peace, but the Allies exacted a harsh punishment.

ANALYZE – The document can be used to support the differences between the views of justice.

CRITICIZE – Brockdorff-Rantzau must return to Germany with the terms of the treaty, so this letter might be more than simply a statement from a disgruntled delegate; it might help him to build the case at home that he did all he could to avoid these harsh terms.

Document F

SUMMARIZE – Clemenceau responds to the German critique in Document E by emphasizing Germany's responsibilities regarding the war. He says that the Allies blame Germany for starting the war and for all of its brutality.

ANALYZE – This document provides evidence to help to explain the differences among the definitions of "just peace."

CRITICIZE – Clemenceau's position is described in Document D, but add to that analysis that here he may also wish to fix blame firmly on the Germans as a means of exculpating the French for their actions.

Document G

SUMMARIZE – The editorial criticizes the peace settlement as too harsh and in violation of Wilson's 14 points.

ANALYZE – The document again gives evidence of a variety of views of justice.

CRITICIZE – A Dutch newspaper might be an objective source of information about the treaty, because the Netherlands remained neutral in the war. It may be a good indication of just how harsh the terms of the treaty were viewed outside of Versailles.

Outside Evidence:

- Self-determination

- Reparations

Possible Categories of Evidence:

- Justice as punishment: D, F, G, reparations

- Humiliation: F, G

- Justice as peace: A, self-determination

- Prepared with terms: C, D

7. DECOLONIZATION

Document A

SUMMARIZE – Gandhi criticizes British rule of India and promises to work for independence.

ANALYZE – The document can be used to support an argument about the view of decolonization from within the colony.

CRITICIZE – It would be difficult for a student who knows much about Gandhi to argue that this interview was in any way self-serving. However, Gandhi may have intended for his words to inspire other Indians to follow his example.

Document B

SUMMARIZE – The statement says that Burma is currently unfit for self-rule and must remain a colony until it can be made ready for independence.

ANALYZE – This document can be used as evidence of at least one reason for resistance against decolonization.

CRITICIZE – This British statement could be an attempt to hold onto the last strands of a dying empire. Why should the British give up this colony if they can convince the rest of the world that they are doing right by the Burmese people?

Document C

SUMMARIZE – Sukarno calls for unity in opposition to colonialism.

ANALYZE – The document is evidence of one view of colonialism and implies a view of decolonization.

CRITICIZE – Sukarno, president of the newly independent Indonesia, could be expected to oppose colonialism and to try to organize other African and Asian independent states to join this view.

Document D

SUMMARIZE – Nehru calls for the nations of Africa and Asia to avoid alignment with the communists or non-communists. He implies that alignment is akin to colonialism.

ANALYZE – The document can be evidence that former colonies oppose anything that even seems colonial.

CRITICIZE – As in Document C, Nehru's view is to be expected from the leader of a newly independent nation.

Document E

SUMMARIZE – The French government affirms its right to organize French colonies in any way it sees fit to improve the financial well-being of France and the colonies.

ANALYZE – The document is evidence of the French view of the legitimacy of colonial rule.

CRITICIZE – Having just lost Vietnam in 1954, France may be trying to avoid further imperial losses by affirming its "honorable" intentions within other French colonies.

Document F

SUMMARIZE – Sadat speaks out against colonialism and calls for opposition from all former colonies.

ANALYZE – The document is evidence of the views of the colonized.

CRITICIZE – Again, as president of a recently independent country, Sadat could be expected to oppose colonialism in any form.

Document G

SUMMARIZE – The UN states that colonialism should end immediately and that a lack of "readiness" is an inadequate argument to delay independence.

ANALYZE – The document shows a widespread view of colonialism.

CRITICIZE – Because France and Britain were both powerful members of the UN in 1960, the passage of this declaration is strong evidence of a shift in world opinion regarding colonialism.

Outside Evidence:

- Salt March

- Statute of Westminster (1931)

Possible Categories of Evidence:

- Support among colonists: A, C, D, F, Salt March

- Opposition outside colonies: B, E, Statute of Westminster

- Necessity: B, E, G

- Alignment is colonization: C, D

8. EUROPEAN UNIFICATION

Document A

SUMMARIZE – Monnet speaks of the ECSC as a first step toward a desired European federation.

ANALYZE – The document can help to explain support of unification.

CRITICIZE – You may recognize Monnet as the architect of the ECSC and, therefore, the document may be his attempt to win adherents. Otherwise, it could be noted that Monnet's statement demonstrates some French support for the ECSC.

Document B

SUMMARIZE – Harriman describes Monnet's proposal as the best progress since the Marshall Plan.

ANALYZE – The document can be used to explain the US view of movement toward unification.

CRITICIZE – The US government would be very concerned in 1950 with the "alignment of Germnay on the side of the West," so Harriman's enthusiasm about Monnet's plan could reflect that more narrow view.

Document C

SUMMARIZE – The treaty strives toward further unification and is supported by Belgium, Germany, France, Italy, Luxembourg, and the Netherlands.

ANALYZE – It may be used to argue for a wider support of unification.

CRITICIZE – If students know the course of European unification, they will be familiar with this treaty as the next step toward the EU after the establishment of the ECSC. The fact that it came soon after the ECSC could be used to argue the strength of the support for further unification.

Document D

SUMMARIZE – De Gaulle argues that political unification is not imminent in Europe.

ANALYZE – The document can be used to explain the reasons cited for opposition to unification.

CRITICIZE – De Gaulle is well known as the French general who refused to give up when his country surrendered to Germany in WWII. It was probably difficult for him to imagine surrendering French autonomy to a European government, especially one that includes Germany.

Document E

SUMMARIZE – Murville seems to explicitly encourage European independence from the U.S.

ANALYZE – This is more evidence of Europe evolving into a single unit.

CRITICIZE – Murville is a member of the De Gaulle government, so he is likely to espouse De Gaulle's nationalist views. Additionally, as Foreign Minister, he may be well aware of the danger for France of becoming entangled in U.S.-Soviet disputes with no French national interest.

Document F

SUMMARIZE – Marjolin says that the opposition to unification is ideological among the Gaullists.

ANALYZE – His statement helps to explain the view of de Gaulle and his followers.

CRITICIZE – Even if you are unaware of Marjolin's efforts to achieve European unity, the title of his book (noted in the citation) may lead you to conclude that he could be expressing bitterness toward those in the French government who blocked the process. The date of publication is also important because he is writing almost 20 years after de Gaulle has left office, so he may be trying to create distance from the Gaullist perspective and make way for new efforts at unity.

Document G

SUMMARIZE – The statement declares that European unification cannot be affected without the hearts and minds of the people of the countries of Europe.

ANALYZE – It provides evidence of one view of unification.

CRITICIZE – The name of the campaign implies the possibility that the statement expresses a pro-labor viewpoint, and may not reflect the views outside the Labor Party.

Outside Evidence:

- UK attitudes toward unification

- European Currency Unit (ECU)

- Eurozone

Possible Categories of Evidence:

- Support of general unity: A, B, C, Eurozone

- Discussion of "Europe" as a concept: E, G, Eurozone

- Support of economic unity: D, ECU, Eurozone

- Opposition to unity: D, F, UK attitudes

Step 3

Part A—
Thesis Recognition

1. CATHOLIC REFORMATION IN SPAIN

A. (2) This thesis addresses all tasks and terms and outlines three clear categories of evidence. Additionally, the author has begun to answer WHY the categories are being used, which makes this thesis particularly analytical.

B. (0) The author has begun to "describe" but has made no attempt to "compare." Therefore, the thesis addresses only some of the tasks and terms.

C. (0) This thesis simply restates the question.

D. (1) Three clear categories of evidence are presented and all tasks and terms are met, but the author has shown very little attempt to analyze the categories. Although, the rest of the first paragraph may fill this void, this score is based solely on the thesis.

E. (0) This thesis fails to address the tasks and terms of the question. The author seems to be heading toward an expository essay about the Counter-Reformation, which would be a misinterpretation of the question.

F. (0) Another restatement of the question.

G. (1) This is basically another version of thesis D.

2. GROWTH OF PARLIAMENTARY POWER IN ENGLAND

A. (0) Although the author mentions the "power" of Parliament, this thesis fails to address the task of discussing the reasons for the growth of that power.

B. (2) This thesis addresses all tasks and terms and begins to analyze three categories of evidence. It may be stated somewhat awkwardly, but the meaning is clear, and grammar and style are not assessed.

C. (1) Again, the grammar in this thesis is lacking, but that is not relevant to the score. There are three categories of evidence and some attempt at analysis.

D. (2) This thesis links its three categories of evidence, not just to the thesis, but also to each other, making it analytical and concise.

E. (0) This one is a bit concerning. It seems to address the "reasons" for Parliament's increased power, but the logic doesn't really hold together. Except for the implication that the victory at Marston Moor increased Parliament's power, the rest merely sets down a chronology of the English Civil War.

F. (0) This one restates the thesis with three simplistic (and meaningless) categories of evidence.

G. (0) Another restatement—this time without even the simplest of categories.

3. ENLIGHTENED DESPOTS

A. (0) This thesis fails to address the terms of the question, which asks about "enlightenment" not "success."

B. (0) Slightly better than the previous thesis, this one addresses the terms but merely restates the question.

C. (1) Despite some very awkward wording, this thesis addresses the tasks and terms and sets up two categories of evidence.

D. (2) This thesis utilizes the dreaded political-social-economic categories, but with sufficient specificity and analysis to warrant a top score.

E. (0) Unlike the previous thesis, this one fails to elaborate on the political-social-economic categories, rendering them too meaningless for a good essay.

F. (2) This thesis is well structured, thorough, and analytical.

G. (2) While it is less well-stated than either D or F, this one certainly addresses the tasks and terms, and it creates three analytical categories of evidence.

4. NAPOLEON AS ANTI-REVOLUTIONARY

A. (1) The author has created a sufficiently strong thesis to earn a point, but there are several problems that may prove fatal to an essay built on this thesis. The "categories" are too specific to yield much evidence, and even with more evidence, this argument will be difficult to make. In fact, with only two categories of evidence, many arguments are logically difficult. Also, be cautious of absolutes like "obviously." AP essay questions rarely lend themselves to "obvious" arguments. Use of words like "obviously" or "clearly" implies a lack of sophistication—an inability to understand the nuances of history.

B. (1) Although this thesis clears the bar of acceptability, it is somewhat problematic because it fails to directly evaluate Napoleon as anti-revolutionary. If you write a thesis of this quality, you will likely create a very strong essay, but you must take care not to get so caught up in describing Napoleon's achievements that you forget to answer the question.

C. (0) This thesis fails to address the tasks and terms of the question, and will very likely result in exactly the kind of essay mentioned above that simply describes Napoleon's achievements.

D. (0) This is just a restatement of the question.

E. (0) Another restatement, and a good example to show that the direction of your answer will not affect the score.

F. (1) This is choice C with the tasks and terms addressed.

G. (2) Better than choice B because it is more analytical, the design of this thesis almost assures that the author will not fall into the trap of listing Napoleon's achievements at the expense of the question itself.

5. INDUSTRIALIZATION AND SOCIAL CHANGE

A. (2) Somewhat awkward at the start, this thesis is clear, logical, and analytical.

B. (1) Overstated! Although overstatement is generally ill-advised on the AP test, with the right evidence and good analysis, this thesis could lend itself to a very nice essay.

C. (0) The structure of this thesis is okay, but the evidence mentioned seems to imply that the author will be writing about the American Industrial Revolution, in which case it will be off-topic.

D. (1) This is a good, concise thesis, and with further analysis in the rest of the opening paragraph, it could yield a top-scoring essay.

E. (1) Although this goes further than restating the question because it states that the lower classes were disadvantaged, the author may have to work very hard to force these generic categories onto this question.

F. (1) This thesis addresses the tasks and terms, but it is very general because it lacks any hint of categories of evidence. It may be, however, a better start than choice E because it does not have to adhere to any contrived categories.

G. (1) This is a very nice thesis. If the author addresses the WHYs of these categories somewhere in the opening paragraph, it could be a good foundation for a top essay.

6. CAUSES OF WORLD WAR I

A. (2) All tasks and terms are addressed, three categories of evidence are clearly stated, and enough analysis is included to demonstrate the logic of this author's thesis.

B. (1) A bit overstated, this thesis establishes three categories of evidence and addresses all tasks and terms, but lacks some of the analysis of choice A.

C. (0) This thesis addresses the "causes" of WWI but fails to mention the author's position on "militarism" as one of them. This author is in danger of misinterpreting the question entirely.

D. (0) This is a restatement of the question.

E. (2) Although it takes a different position than choice A, this thesis is equally well-written.

F. (2) The most thorough of these choices, this one may not be as fluid as A or E but it is more analytical.

G. (0) Even though this author replaced "social" with "militarism," these categories need more analysis to be useful.

7. IMPORTANCE OF THE MARSHALL PLAN

A. (0) This thesis is a restatement of the question.

B. (2) This is a great thesis; however, the author may have some trouble supporting the first two categories because much of the necessary evidence may be statistics.

C. (1) Basically a chronology, this thesis could be supported with the right evidence, but will most likely result in an expository essay.

D. (2) By introducing Shuman and Monnet, this author demonstrates a superior knowledge of the period, and if he/she can produce the evidence to back up these claims, this promises to be an excellent essay. The thesis itself is well structured and at least partially analytical.

E. (1) The thesis warrants the point, but this author seems to be a bit preachy, which is really not a good thing on an AP LEQ because it can drive an essay off-topic.

F. (1) Although the author utilizes the now-infamous political-social-economic categories, they are analyzed just well enough to make for an acceptable argument.

G. (0) Sometimes structure isn't enough—this student needed a better grasp of the content.

8. EUROPE'S COMMON CURRENCY

A. (2) By now, I hope a great thesis is fairly obvious to you.

B. (0) This is a classic. The author has packaged a restatement of the question so that it almost looks like it is saying something new. Again, you should be capable of recognizing the restatement by this time.

C. (1) This one may still be a tough call for many students. It lacks a third category, but that alone may not diminish the score. Besides the third category, the only thing missing from this thesis is any sign of analysis—a weakness that could be corrected within the opening paragraph.

D. (0) No strong essay is likely to begin with this sentence, but it is certainly more than a restatement. One solid category of evidence is established, which is insufficient for a balanced analysis, but could earn the point for a historically defensible claim.

E. (0) Social, political, economic—enough said.

F. (0) Although this author might surprise the reader with a brief discussion of the favorable arguments demanded by the tasks and terms, it is much more likely that this essay will focus entirely on the negative arguments and, thus, misinterpret the question.

G. (2) This thesis uses national categories, which are perfectly acceptable in this case. Additionally, you should recognize the author's analysis—raising this example to the top.

Step
3

Part B—
Analytical Thesis Development

1. ORIGINS OF CHRISTIAN HUMANISM

Tasks: "Assess the extent"

Terms: "Christian Humanism," "roots," "Italian Humanists"

Question restated: In what ways was Christian Humanism rooted in Italian Humanism? In what ways was Christian Humanism NOT rooted in Italian Humanism?

Sample Thesis: To the extent that Christian Humanists believed in the power of man to understand his world (and his faith) without the intervention of academic and religious authorities, and they developed their philosophies based on the study of Italian Humanist thought, Christian Humanism was rooted in Italian Humanism. To the extent, however, that they were detached from Roman antiquity both culturally and geographically, their Christian focus was not rooted in Italian Humanism.

2. THE ROMAN CATHOLIC CHURCH AND ASTRONOMY

Tasks: "Analyze"

Terms: "impact of Roman Catholic doctrine," "study of astronomy," "16th and 17th centuries"

Question restated: In what ways or for what reasons was the study of astronomy affected by Roman Catholic doctrine between 1500 and 1700?

Sample Thesis: Because astronomical theory was so closely linked to theology, many of the earliest astronomers were actually Churchmen, and Christian faith superseded all other beliefs in the minds of Europeans at the time, Roman Catholic doctrine impacted the study of astronomy in the 16th and 17th centuries.

3. ENLIGHTENMENT OPTIMISM

Tasks: "To what extent"

Terms: "ideas of the Enlightenment," "optimism about humanity"

Question Restated: In what ways were Enlightenment ideas optimistic about humanity? In what ways were Enlightenment ideas NOT optimistic about humanity?

Sample Graphic Organizer:

Enlightment Ideas	Underlying Assumptions about People
Popular sovereignty	People are capable of self-government. Popular sovereignty will be good for all. People are generally good-willed. Rule by the people is better than monarchy.
Faith in human reason	People can solve problems through reason.
Deism	God is not needed after creation. God is satisfied that man could be trusted. People do not need organized religion.

Enlightment Ideas	Underlying Assumptions about People
Social contract	People must sacrifice some liberty to enjoy government protection. Governments must
Social justice	People must adhere to a natural order. All people are endowed with some inalienable rights.

In what ways is it TRUE? People are generally good and trustworthy (popular sovereignty, deism, reason). People are capable (popular sovereignty, reason, deism).

In what ways is it FALSE? Individuals may be bad leaders (popular sovereignty, social contract). Those in power may not always protect the interests of the group (popular sovereignty, deism, social contract, social justice).

> *Sample Thesis:* To the extent that self-government, human reason, and deism were based on assumptions of human goodness and ability, Enlightenment ideas were expressions of optimism about humanity. Because, however, notions of popular sovereignty, deism, social contract, and social justice were developed in opposition to tyrannies, it seems that Enlightenment ideas were not very optimistic about people in power.

4. CONGRESS OF VIENNA

> *Tasks:* "Analyze the ways"
>
> *Terms:* "Congress of Vienna," "conservative political theory," "create stability," "post-Napoleonic Europe"
>
> *Question Restated:* How did the Congress of Vienna use conservatism to create stability after 1815? Why did they use these methods? Were these methods successful?
>
> *Sample Thesis:* By focusing on the excesses of liberalism and the evils of the French Revolution, and stereotyping all proponents of liberalism according to the traits of their extremist minority, the leaders of the Congress of Vienna were able to create a stable Europe based on the conservative principles of the old monarchies.

5. UNIFICATION OF ITALY AND GERMANY

Tasks: "Compare," "contrast"

Terms: "influence of nationalism," "Italian unification," "German unification"

Question Restated: In what ways or for what reasons was the effect of nationalism on Italian and German unification the same? In what ways or for what reasons was the effect of nationalism on Italian and German unification different?

Sample Thesis: In both Italy and Germany, government officials, interested in unification for their own purposes, were able to use a popular spirit of nationalism to create unified kingdoms. German officials, however, were able to maintain control of this popular movement, whereas their Italian counterparts were barely able to keep up with the nationalist surge.

6. INTERWAR ART

Tasks: "To what extent"

Terms: "art," "interwar," "reaction to WWI"

Question Restated: In what ways did art react to WWI between 1918 and 1939? In what ways did art NOT react to WWI between 1918 and 1939?

Sample Thesis: To the extent that Irrationalism in literature and the visual arts grew out of the disillusionment in the rational ideas that allowed for such massive destruction, interwar art was driven by reaction to World War I; to the extent, however, that many Lost Generation writers and painters used prewar techniques to make political statements, interwar art was more evolution than revolution.

7. WWII CONFERENCES AND COLD WAR POLICY

Tasks: "Analyze"

Terms: "impact of WWII allied conferences," "cold war policy"

Question Restated: In what ways or for what reasons was cold war policy effected by WWII allied conferences?

Sample Thesis: The exclusion of the Soviets from the earliest Allied conferences and the animosity between Stalin and Churchill fueled an East-West mutual distrust, exacerbated by an American diplomacy that avoided direct confrontation among the Allies, would become a hallmark of cold war policy.

8. ANTI-SOVIET UPRISINGS IN EASTERN EUROPE

Tasks: "Discuss"

Terms: "reasons for successes," "reasons for failures," "anti-Soviet uprisings," "Eastern Europe," "1950-1989"

Question Restated: In what ways and for what reasons did anti-Soviet uprisings succeed in Eastern Europe between 1950 and 1989? In what ways and for what reasons did anti-Soviet uprisings fail in Eastern Europe between 1950 and 1989?

Sample Thesis: Anti-Soviet uprisings of the 1950s and 60s failed to break free of Soviet domination because the nuclear threat of the cold war prevented overt Western assistance for the rebels and the suppression of Soviet dissent was sufficiently strong to hide the realities of these uprisings from the masses. After the 1970s, however, the combination of glasnost within the Soviet Union and reduced nuclear threat globally permitted greater opposition to Soviet oppression and the eventual end of the Soviet satellite system.

Step 4 Presenting the Argument

1. CATHOLIC REFORMATION IN SPAIN

Sample Opening Paragraph: Among the components of the Catholic Reformation in Spain were the Jesuits, who worked through education and conversion; the Inquisition, which operated through fear; and the monarchy, which used conquest and royal edict to conduct Reformation activities. While the Society of Jesus reached out to find new converts and teach them the ways of Christianity, the Dominicans sought to root out heretics from within. With the support of Ferdinand and Isabella, these two religious orders expanded and cleansed the ranks of the faithful in Spain.

2. GROWTH OF PARLIAMENTARY POWER IN ENGLAND

Sample Opening Paragraph: Like their Tudor predecessor, the Stuart kings incurred a heavy debt and needed Parliament's help to raise funds. Unlike Elizabeth, however, James I and Charles I abused their royal prerogative and failed to recognize their own precarious position. At each misstep, Parliament used the opportunity to wrestle more power from the monarchy. This evolution took a giant leap forward when Parliament defeated Charles I in military conflict, and later negotiated a Glorious Revolution with William and Mary. Heavy war debt, which led to a need for Parliament's approval of more taxes; the monarchy's refusal to negotiate with Parliament, which led to a military engagement and regicide; and the willingness of William and Mary to accept Parliament's invitation to the throne in 1688, which formalized Parliament's claims to power, combined to extend the power of Parliament in England 1625–1688.

3. ENLIGHTENED DESPOTS

Sample Opening Paragraph: Even before the French Revolution, Prussia instituted its own progressive law code. Hailed by the likes of Voltaire, Frederick's new law established an unparalleled legal equality and religious freedom. Unfortunately, as Voltaire himself discovered, Frederick was more interested in strengthening the monarchy than in instituting reform. Joseph, although he was too weak to maintain his reforms, may have been one of just a few monarchs of his century who believed in them. To the extent that the Prussian Code instituted equality before the law and religious freedom, the reign of Frederick the Great was more enlightened than that of Joseph II, but to the extent that Joseph's reforms were enacted for the sake of reforming Austrian society, while Frederick acted primarily to enhance the power of the monarchy, Frederick was less enlightened than Joseph.

4. NAPOLEON AS ANTI-REVOLUTIONARY

Sample Opening Paragraph: To the extent that Napoleon I ruled with almost absolute power, he had violated the principles of popular sovereignty on which much of the revolution had been built; however, to the extent that, even as an absolutist, Napoleon often acted in the interests of the French people, and the Napoleonic Code edified many of the legal reforms begun earlier in the revolution, he was not at all anti-revolutionary. Even during the Consulate, Napoleon's will was generally unimpeded, but this absolutism did not diminish his image with the French public. Frenchmen loved Napoleon because, unlike his republican predecessors, he solved the problems of French society and even completed many of the reforms begun in the revolution.

5. INDUSTRIALIZATION AND SOCIAL CHANGE

Sample Opening Paragraph: As a result of the Industrial Revolution, lower-class families were broken down because all members of the family needed to work outside the home; lower-class children were less educated because their families needed them to work from a very young age; and lower-class women were often driven to prostitution because it paid more than factory work. While farmers were able to maintain traditional family dynamics, many of the urban poor were forced to abandon traditional lifestyles for the sake of economic survival. Because every member of the family was often forced to work long hours outside the home, lower-class children remained uneducated and young girls, sometimes alone and uneducated in the city, resorted to prostitution to make ends meet.

6. CAUSES OF WORLD WAR I

Sample Opening Paragraph: To the extent that the great powers were engaged in an arms race that resulted in new weapons on land and at sea, and France and Germany each developed plans to destroy the other on the battlefield, militarism was a major cause of World War I; however, to the extent that the arms race and war games were the result of the hubris and short-sightedness of the leaders of these nations, militarism was merely a byproduct. Germany and Britain, competing with each other for naval supremacy, each welcomed the opportunity to prove their prowess in battle. Expecting a conflict of massive proportions, French military officials and their German counterparts had destroyed each other several times over on paper, but what made all these preparations so deadly was the fact that every great power in 1914 believed itself too strong to be defeated and imagined no circumstance under which they could achieve anything except a quick victory.

7. IMPORTANCE OF THE MARSHALL PLAN

Sample Opening Paragraph: Because Marshall Plan monies amounted to only about 5% of Western Europe's GNP and several countries had already achieved prewar production levels by 1948, the Marshall Plan was not essential to European recovery; however, the fact that Marshall Plan rules required the cooperation of European nations and helped to inspire the formation of the ECSC, which led to the EU, the Marshall Plan can be said to have maximized long-term growth in postwar Europe. Marshall Plan monies amounted to such a small portion of the total recovery effort that several nations almost refused the assistance. In fact, France was one of a few countries that had already exceeded its prewar production levels. Ultimately, however, it may be the legacy of the European Coal & Steel Community, inspired by Marshall Plan rules, that most changed Europe after World War II, transforming it eventually into one of the world's most dominant economic powers.

8. EUROPE'S COMMON CURRENCY

Sample Opening Paragraph: Prior to the Euro, travelers and businesses throughout Europe were forced to pay exchange surcharges at every border, amounting to millions in fees that could be eliminated with a common currency. Although several national currencies had performed well on the global market, the "gold standard" continued to be the US dollar—that was expected to change with the introduction of the Euro. With hundreds of millions of people doing business with the common currency, it was expected to gain strength against the dollar and develop a stability that was previously unknown in Europe, lowering interest rates and inspiring growth. Those in favor of adopting the Euro argued that a single currency would save each nation millions of dollars in exchange fees, that a currency used by all Europeans would be much more stable and so compete well with the almighty dollar, and that the added stability would tend to lower interest rates within Europe, thereby promoting further growth.

Step 5
Part A—Analyzing Evidence for the Long Essay

1. ELIZABETHAN ENGLAND

Sample Thesis: To the extent that Elizabeth I, a Protestant, focused more on the state than on religious disputes, she can be described as religiously tolerant; however, when provoked by extremists that threatened her life or her throne, Elizabeth acted intolerantly to preserve her crown and the stability of her state.

Sample Body Paragraph: Elizabeth said, "There is only one Christ, Jesus, one faith . . . all else is a dispute over trifles." Although some have accused her of being an atheist, it may be more accurate to say that she cared more for her throne than for her faith. She encouraged her subjects to believe whatever they wanted but to always remain loyal to England. In fact, it was disloyalty that eventually provoked her to attack some Catholics and the Roman Church. The rebellion, which was led by Mary Queen of Scots and supported by the pope's excommunication of Elizabeth, led the queen to institute a series of measures aimed at limiting the power and freedom of Catholics in England. Her distrust of Catholics grew throughout the 1570s and 80s, and it eventually manifested itself in a struggle against Philip of Spain that ended with England's defeat of the Spanish Armada.

2. THEORIES OF ASTRONOMY

Sample Thesis: In pursuit of a better understanding of the universe and the laws that govern it, scientists developed mechanistic theories that advanced the fields of physics, biology, and chemistry.

Sample Body Paragraph: As scientists moved away from geocentric theories of the universe, the specifics of heliocentrism became the focus. Johann Kepler, using the notes of Tycho Brahe, developed a mathematical theory to describe how elliptical orbits could explain the anomaly of retrograde movement of the stars. Brahe's star charts later helped scientists struggling with the longitude problem, but the key to future studies was Isaac Newton's perfection of the mechanistic theory of the universe. Newton's Laws inspired scientists in many fields to seek reasonable explanations for longtime problems. If the universe could be explained through predictable mathematical equations, then perhaps other branches of science, like biology or chemistry, were equally mechanistic.

3. ROOTS OF SOCIAL CONTRACT THEORIES

Sample Thesis: The social contract theory of Thomas Hobbes was influenced by events of the English Civil war, including the execution of Charles I and the "crowning" of the Lord Protector; whereas John Locke's writing was shaped by events of the Glorious Revolution.

Sample Body Paragraph: Unlike the disorderly events that most influenced the writing of Thomas Hobbes, the Glorious Revolution impressed John Locke as a most orderly turn of events. Where Hobbes had witnessed veritable mob rule in the 1640s, Locke's experience was one of civility and relative calm. King James II, despised by those around him, stepped down without a fight at the approach of William's army. William and Mary, in turn, assumed the throne with the understanding that they would share power with Parliament, as had been previously agreed. Locke would have certainly admired the way "the people" managed to peacefully change governments, and the way the monarchs abided by their "contract" with the people of England.

These events helped Locke to spin his version of the social contract with a lot more optimism than his predecessor.

4. FRENCH REVOLUTION AND WOMEN

Sample Thesis: Women of the Third Estate often joined their male counterparts in the ground-level revolution, while a few upper class women contributed directly to the ideas and activities of key revolutionary figures.

Sample Body Paragraph: While women of the Second Estate did not participate in the revolution en masse, there are several outstanding examples of women acting individually for the cause. Madame de Stael, daughter of Jacques Necker, hosted one of the most famous salons in France. Through her, and women like her, the greatest minds of the revolution were brought together to exchange ideas. Although most of the formal political planning was done within the walls of many clubs (Feuillant, Cordelier, Jacobin, etc.), these meetings were often composed of single-minded men. It was only at the salons that men (and women) of many ideologies were able to mingle peacefully and politely.

5. REVOLUTIONS OF 1848

Sample Thesis: In the sense that several groups of revolutionaries established new governments, at least temporarily, and Europeans began to accept that nationalism and liberalism would not be suppressed, the Revolutions of 1848 were successful; however, because none of these revolutionaries managed to hold onto their power for very long, the uprisings were, largely, unsuccessful.

Sample Body Paragraph: Although the reigning monarchs in many cases were never dethroned, in several countries, revolutionary governments were established for a time. Liberals in Prussia set up the Frankfurt Assembly and offered a constitutional German throne to the Hohenzollern family. Had Frederick accepted the offer and placed the Prussian army between himself and those who opposed him, the Frankfurt Assembly may have succeeded. In Italy, nationalist revolutionaries, led by Giuseppe Mazzini, established the first Roman Republic since antiquity. Unfortunately, Mazzini's opposition was still too strong in 1848 and the Republic soon fell. The momentum of Mazzini's nationalist revolution was sufficient, however, to draw support, if only for his own reasons, from Camille di Cavour of Piedmont-Sardinia, who would eventually accept nationalism as essential to the unification of Italy.

6. IMPACT OF TECHNOLOGY 1900–1918

Sample Thesis: New technology helped to spur on the militarism that preceded the Great War, and new weapons shifted the military advantage to the defense and ultimately created the means by which over 30 million men would be lost in the war.

Sample Body Paragraph: Although the militarism of the early 20th century was motivated, at least in part, by the nationalism of the time period, it was certainly accelerated by new technology. Advances in steel manufacture allowed for improvements in naval vessels, armored vehicles, and artillery weapons. The Anglo-German race to build bigger and better navies, symbolized by the dreadnought, exemplifies the impact of steel technology on the war effort. In fact, it was this naval race that led Germany to explore submarine technology and create a weapon that would ultimately draw the United States into the Great War. In addition to naval developments, new technology improved land warfare through newer and better guns, including larger rifled artillery weapons and machine guns, the latter of which was perhaps most responsible for shifting the advantage to the defensive army.

7. ECONOMIC IMPACT OF WORLD WAR II

Sample Thesis: The destruction caused by WWII created a postwar demand for new housing which, in turn, helped Britain's postwar economy grow, but the biggest reason for Europe's postwar boom may have been the influence of the Marshall Plan and the military buildup associated with NATO.

Sample Body Paragraph: While a housing shortage may have added to the growth of European economies outside of Britain as well, probably the biggest impact on continental economies was the Marshall Plan. Western Europe was in dire need of foreign investment in the months immediately following the war, and US money satisfied that need. More importantly, however, Marshall Plan money came with strict rules for economic cooperation and organization. Formerly disparate nations were forced to work cooperatively to break down trade barriers and stimulate growth across the western continent. France and Germany, former enemy combatants, formed the core of Monnet's European Coal and Steel Community, which would evolve later into the EU. Additionally, the Marshall Plan required cooperation between labor and business within participating nations. The US was loath to provoke new Soviet-style "workers' revolts," so labor had to agree to moderate pay raises and businesses had to agree to moderate profits. This cooperation helped to create the successful mixed-economies of the 1950s and 60s. If not for the exhaustion of resources resulting from WWII, Western Europe would have had no reason to seek US aid and, therefore, no reason to install Marshall Plan policies.

8. EVOLUTION OF THE EUROPEAN UNION

Sample Thesis: Since France and Germany were at the heart of the original European Coal and Steel Community (ECSC) and France has largely become the dominant member of the EU, Britain's decisions are a bit marginalized; however, French domination was caused, in part, by Britain's decision to stay out of the ECSC and, even after Britain joined the EC, to retain its currency as separate from the Euro.

Sample Body Paragraph: The motivation for the original European Coal and Steel Community was to break down the barriers between the two greatest continental economies—France and Germany. From the beginning, French officials were in a position to establish the direction of ECSC policies. As the ECSC evolved into the European Economic Community, France continued to dominate policy decisions that affected all the members. When Britain sought admission to the EEC in the 1970s, it was Gaullist France that dictated the terms of the expansion. Of course, much of the reason behind this French domination was the fact that Britain refused to join the community earlier in its development, wishing to remain unencumbered by continental constraints.

Step 5

Part B—Analyzing Evidence for the DBQ

1. BAROQUE ART

Sample Thesis: Baroque artists of Italy and the Netherlands differed in their use of color and shadow, as well as their choice of subjects.

Sample Body Paragraph: Beyond color and shadow, the biggest difference between Baroque artists in Italy and the Netherlands was their choice of subjects. Caravaggio, whose use of light and shadow is most like that of Dutch artists, focused almost exclusively on biblical subjects like *The Supper at Emmaus* (Document A). In contrast, Rembrandt chose contemporary, even commonplace, subjects for most of his works. In fact, *The Money Changer*, based on the "Parable of the Rich Fool," is one of the few exceptions (Document D). His other paintings are more like Rubens' *The Night Watch*, depicting the Dutch Arquebusiers. In fact, Dutch focus on contemporary subjects led to Sandrart's criticism that Rembrandt's problem is that he lacked a "knowledge of Italy" (Document F).

2. SPANISH LITERATURE

Sample Thesis: Spanish writers of the Golden Age rejected the grandeur and superhuman characters of the chivalric epics, but these same characteristics are often evident in their own works.

Sample Body Paragraph: Although Juan Luis Vives was one of those who explicitly criticized the chivalric epics, the influences of the style are evident in his description of the "honest woman" as "silent and modest," like those helpless damsels in the old chivalric stories (Document B). Góngora's "Ode to the Armada" also reflects the influence of these past epics in its grandiose descriptions and tributes to the great kings of old (Document C). If Góngora's motivation was religious, however, it might be possible that his glorious language was genuinely inspired by his Catholic faith. The values of chivalry were still evident in works of the seventeenth century, like "The Star of Seville," in which Carpio features a king expressing chivalric love for a woman in a window (Document G). Of course, without the rest of the dialogue excerpted in this document, it is impossible to know if the king is a hero or villain, in which case his words may be a mockery of chivalric love. In the same century, Pedro Calderón de la Barca writes of a love so great that the speaker would trade his soul for the woman (Document H).

3. MOZART

Sample Thesis: To the extent that Mozart was influenced by Rousseau, an Enlightenment thinker, his music can be seen as an extension of the Enlightenment, but because Rousseau's focus on emotions broke from the Enlightenment emphasis on reason, and Mozart seems to have been drawn to that particular theme, his works might be seen as reactions to the Enlightenment.

Sample Body Paragraph: Even bigger than his influence on the French Revolution was Rousseau's impact on the reaction to that revolution—the Romantic Era. It was his emphasis on the importance of emotion over reason that inspired the post-revolutionary period, and it was emotion that captured the attention of Mozart. In fact, Mozart explicitly disavows reason as a source of genius when he writes that true genius comes from "love, love, love" (Document F). His works seemed to have been created to affect the senses rather than the mind. Niemetschek notes this point in his review of *Tito* (Document G). Rather than appealing to human reason, Mozart seems to have been working to evoke an emotional response in his audience.

4. ART OF REVOLUTION

Sample Thesis: Art of the late 18th and early 19th centuries reflected the French Revolution's Enlightenment ideals of equality and reason, but, unlike the French Revolutionaries' focus on ancient subjects, artists often limited their work to ancient forms.

Sample Body Paragraph: In contrast to David's exceptional *Death of Socrates*, more often, artists of the revolutionary period adhered to ancient forms while avoiding ancient subjects (Document B). Percier and Fontaine designed the *Arc de Triomphe du Carrousel* to pay tribute to the French army in the style of the ancient Romans (Document D). It must be noted, however, that this monument was commissioned by Napoleon I, who is known to have imagined himself like a Roman emperor. Vignon created La Madeleine to resemble the ancient Parthenon, but, envisioned first as a tribute to the Grand Army, it later became a church (Document E). David himself often shied away from ancient subjects as in one of his most famous images, *Bonaparte Crossing the St. Bernard Pass*, which depicts the emperor in a typically heroic pose (Document C).

5. ART OF THE ROMANTIC ERA

Sample Thesis: If Baroque artists reflected Enlightenment ideals, then Romanticism differed because of its emphasis on emotion and nature rather than reason, as seen in poetry and the visual arts.

Sample Body Paragraph: Emotion was also the focus of many works of visual art. Goya's *Executions of the Third of May* portrayed the tragic brutality experienced by the Spanish at the hands of Napoleon and the French army (Document D). Despite their earlier attraction to Enlightenment ideals, many Spanish artists expressed disillusionment with the outcome of the French Revolution. Théodore Géricault's *Raft of the Medusa* depicts another tragic scene created by the French (Document E). The painting shows the horrors faced by Algerian immigrants shipwrecked off the African coast. It evoked so much emotion that it was criticized as a political attack on the government of France.

6. POST-ROMANTIC REALISM

Sample Thesis: The characteristics of works of 19th-century Realism include a focus on details and everyday scenes, and a rejection of perfect forms.

Sample Body Paragraph: Detailed portrayals of everyday scenes can also be viewed as a rejection of perfect forms. Whereas the portraiture of earlier artists would have depicted a subject posed in an ideal setting, Manet's *Portrait of Émile Zola* shows the subject at work at a messy desk (Document D). Degas' *The Cotton Exchange at New Orleans* shows a cluttered room full of people, with no attempt at glorifying the scene (Document F). Degas seems to have found beauty in the imperfection of reality. He claims to have been attracted to "everything" (Document E). The rejection of perfection is most evident in Henrick Ibsen's *An Enemy of the People* when he associates worn trousers with freedom and truth (Document G).

7. EXPRESSIONISM

Sample Thesis: Expressionism was seen as an internal worldview, unconventional in form and focused wholly on the essence of the subject.

Sample Body Paragraph: The visible characteristics of Expressionist art derive from the fact that it originates from within the artist. Images like Marc's *The Tower of Blue Horses* make no real attempt to depict the external reality, but rather try to bring to life some internal view of the world (Document B). Although, given Marc's own words in 1914, he was actually trying to be unconventional, no matter where his art originates (Document D). Other artists, however, support the idea that their art originates from within. Wassily Kandinsky writes explicitly that Expressionism comes from within—art is "created by the vibration of the soul" (Document C). Herwarth Walden agrees that artists "have art" within them (Document E). Despite Marc's comments, it may be that Expressionist art depicted an internal worldview.

8. POSTMODERNISM

Sample Thesis: Postmodernism is an attempt to break down the structures of the past and create a new "unstructured" reality, while recognizing that this new reality is limited by its rejection of the past and its own self-definition.

Sample Body Paragraph: Despite the postmodernist's attempt to create a new "unstructured" reality, he is always conscious of the limitations placed on him by his own definition of the new reality. Trilling, in *The Liberal Imagination*, concedes that thinking is flawed because it is constrained by ideas (Document A). If the postmodernist tries to imagine the new reality, he will be limited by his own ideas. According to Foster, even if the postmodernist tries to break free of the ideas of the past, his artistic reaction will be inexorably tied to the tradition he has rejected (Document B). Michael Dear tries to explain the whole conundrum by declaring that definitions of postmodernism are, in themselves, modernist structures (Document D).

Step 5

Part C— Analytical Transitions

1. COLUMBIAN EXCHANGE

Sample Thesis: To the extent that plants and animals were exchanged to the benefit of both worlds, the Columbian Exchange was mutually beneficial; however, because the Native Americans were forced to abandon their beliefs for Christianity and afflicted with several European diseases, the Europeans gained a greater advantage from the exchange.

Sample Transition: Despite the long-term benefits to both hemispheres, the immediate impact of the Columbian Exchange held harsh repercussions for the Native Americans.

2. APPLICATIONS OF DIVINE RIGHT THEORY

Sample Thesis: France and England both employed divine right theory to justify absolutism, but while French policy was shaped to make the monarchy more effective, royal policy in England tended only to aggravate an already difficult relationship between the king and the nobility.

Sample Transition: Unlike Bourbon policies that tended to enhance the power of the king in France, Stuart policies of the 17th century created greater tension between the king and the nobility.

3. SKEPTICISM AND WITCHCRAFT

Sample Thesis: While most defenders of the existence of witchcraft relied on tradition and Church doctrine to justify their beliefs, their opponents depended most heavily on reason to make their arguments.

Sample Transition: Traditional beliefs about witchcraft were sometimes supported by misconstrued interpretations of Church doctrine.

4. ROBESPIERRE AS AN IDEALIST

Sample Thesis: Although Robespierre is viewed most often as the dictatorial architect of the Terror, because of his devotion to Rousseau's philosophy and his strict adherence to the value of human liberty, he may be the most idealistic proponent of Enlightenment ideas among the French revolutionaries.

Sample Transition: Despite the thousands of Frenchmen who died at the guillotine, Robespierre's actions may be mitigated by his devotion to the philosophy of Rousseau.

5. BOER WARS

Sample Thesis: Published works of the early 20th century portrayed the British army in the Boer Wars as patriotic and courageous, but the same sources often criticized the war effort as ill guided and unnecessary.

Sample Transition: Many of the same sources that praised the British soldier for his courage criticized the war effort for its wrong-headedness.

6. GERMAN AMBITIONS AND WORLD WAR I

Sample Thesis: To the extent that Germany's goals of dominating continental affairs and building the world's strongest military ended in conflict with France and Britain, the Kaiser shares much of the responsibility for starting the war; but to the extent that Britain's own military ambitions helped fuel the arms race and France's military arrogance negated the possibility for prewar negotiations, Germany was no more guilty than the other great powers.

Sample Transition: Like Britain's military ambitions in the early 20th century, French military arrogance contributed to a scenario in which war was almost inevitable.

7. SCIENCES IN POST-WWII SOVIET RUSSIA

Sample Thesis: Stalin's determination to prove the superiority of Soviet economic and political policy led to the creation of a scientific community intent on winning his approval at the expense of good science, and subsequent theories based on Soviet presuppositions and unsupported by research.

Sample Transition: As the scientific community became more and more obsequious, the scientific theories it generated evolved into little more than unsupported Soviet presuppositions.

8. SOVIET DECLINE AND UNIFICATION OF EUROPE

Sample Thesis: The decline and eventual end of the Soviet Union and the Soviet bloc invigorated the European unification movement by opening more countries to membership in the EU, inspiring greater European unity by breaking down the unnatural division between western and eastern nations, and removing the cold war threat that had been the reason for heavy US participation in European affairs.

Sample Transition: In addition to helping create greater unity among European nations in the east and west, Soviet decline created a more relaxed geopolitical atmosphere within which the US was no longer needed as a dominant player.

Step 6
Effective Closing Paragraphs

1. PROTESTANT AND CATHOLIC REFORMATION

Sample Thesis: The Protestant movement of the 16th century grew out of a general dissatisfaction with the Church's practices of simony, absenteeism and pluralism, and its apparent focus on earthly wealth. In its 17th-century response, although the Roman Catholic Church reaffirmed its basic doctrines, Church officials reformed the offending practices.

Sample Closing Paragraph: Through the Council of Trent and the efforts of individual popes of the 17th century, the Roman Catholic Church indirectly answered the Protestant call for reform. The practices of simony, absenteeism, and pluralism were discontinued and procedures were put in place to encourage Church officials to live more spiritually. Protestant demands for reformed Church doctrine, however, were absolutely rejected as the Church reinforced the doctrines of transubstantiation and papal infallibility. The Roman Catholic Church of the 17th century, inspired at least in part by the 16th-century Protestant movement, reformed offensive practices like simony, absenteeism, and pluralism, encouraged its clergy to focus more attention on spirituality than on secular affairs, but refused to alter basic Church doctrine.

2. RUSSIAN TIME OF TROUBLES

Sample Thesis: Political instability during the Russian Time of Troubles was the result of social disorder, contention for the throne, and external pressures created by Polish aggression.

Sample Closing Paragraph: The 17th century opened in Russia with social disorder characterized by "hundreds of corpses" daily. Social chaos was exasperated by political disorder resulting from at least two pretenders to the throne over a twenty-year period. To further exasperate the troubles, during all this internal conflict, the Kingdom of Poland assailed Russia. The threat of Polish conquest, combined with social and political upheaval, resulted in the period of Russian history known as the Time of Troubles.

3. ROOTS OF DEISM

Sample Thesis: The basic tenets of Deism established a divine being who created the world and set the wheels in motion, but who remained uninvolved in everyday affairs. This mechanistic view of creation perfectly mirrored the theories of the universe put forth by Galileo and Newton, and adhered to the logical principles of the scientific method.

Sample Closing Paragraph: Galileo, using the skill of observation, theorized that the universe operated according to predictable movements. Newton later developed mathematical formulas to support Galileo's theory, developing the Laws of Motion that "ruled" physics for two centuries. Galileo, Newton, and others of the Scientific Revolution recognized disconnect between the universe created by their theories and the one created in the Bible. Since many of these thinkers were also devout Christians, they searched for ways to reconcile their theories with their faith. They envisioned a predictable universe, created by God, but operating independent of any supreme being. This new "religion," Deism, reflected the theories of Galileo and Newton, and adhered to the standards of the scientific method.

4. SEARCH FOR LONGITUDE

Sample Thesis: The scientific elite of the 17th and 18th centuries generally sought a longitude solution using star charts and the mechanics of the universe, while a few independent inventors worked to solve the problem with clocks. Though both solutions eventually found some success, the clock offered the simplest and most reliable solution.

Sample Closing Paragraph: Isaac Newton, one of the most well respected members of the scientific community, used his considerable clout to support an astronomical solution to the longitude problem. He and several other scientists criticized John Harrison's clock as impractical at sea. Despite many setbacks, including the criticism of Newton and his followers, Harrison persisted in improving his chronometer until it proved itself a worthy solution. Although star charts were also successfully used in future navigation, it was the clock that gave the simplest and most reliable solution.

5. VICTORIAN SOCIETY

Sample Thesis: Victorian society is perhaps best remembered for its prudery, but England in the late 1800s was also a nation of industrious, self-disciplined middle class families, whose diligence and sobriety propelled the industrial revolution.

Sample Closing Paragraph: The stiff collars and corseted dresses of Victorian England stand as examples of the prudish attitudes of its citizens. Although this stereotype may prove accurate on the surface, the underlying qualities of the English middle class were much more important to the age. Middle class families possessed an industry and self-discipline that led even poorer citizens to regard them as models. Their diligence and sobriety produced an age of industrial growth and innovation exemplified by the success of the Great Exposition of 1851.

6. BREST-LITOVSK NEGOTIATIONS

Sample Thesis: The new Russian leaders in 1917 withdrew from WWI for practical and ideological reasons, but the responses were purely practical—the Central Powers unanimously supported the withdrawal while the Allies uniformly opposed the move.

Sample Closing Paragraph: Russia had been losing badly since the start of the Great War and popular reaction to the losses contributed to a general sense that the czar was leading poorly. The Russian army's poor performance helped the Bolsheviks to overthrow Czar Nicholas and gain a share of state power. Popular discontent with the war combined with the new socialist anti-war ideology of the Bolshevik government and led to Russia's withdrawal. The Germans and their allies reacted to Russia's appeal with open arms, because it provided them a way out of their two-front war. Since the Russian withdrawal would allow the Central Powers to devote all their attention to the Western Front, the Allies adamantly opposed the Brest-Litovsk Treaty. Although the new Russian government withdrew from WWI for a combination of practical and ideological reasons, the Allied and Axis responses were purely practical.

7. SOVIET OPPOSITION IN EASTERN EUROPE

Sample Thesis: To the extent that challenges to Soviet domination in East Germany, Poland, and Hungary were squashed by the Soviet military, the opposition movements were unsuccessful; however, to the extent that the new Communist leaders in Poland and Hungary were able to gradually liberalize their governments and the Soviet leadership was too busy with its own domestic affairs to notice this liberalization, the opposition movements were successful in breaking down Soviet domination of the region.

Sample Closing Paragraph: The 1950s opposition movements in East Germany, Poland, and Hungary that threatened the unity of the Warsaw Pact and Soviet domination of Eastern Europe were met with harsh Soviet military reprisals. Opposition leaders were executed, and thousands of reform-minded citizens fled to Western Europe. Although the East German uprising resulted in an even more repressive government, challenges to Soviet power in Poland and Hungary led eventually to more liberal leaders and weakened Soviet control. These reforms were as much a result of Soviet internal conflicts, including anti-Khrushchev challenges from within the Communist Party, as they were the result of the political skill of the new Polish and Hungarian leaders. Despite the immediate failure of 1950s anti-Soviet rebellions in Eastern Europe, the subsequent success of more liberal leaders in those same countries combined with the distraction of Soviet internal troubles helped lead to an overall decline in Soviet domination of the Eastern Bloc.

8. 21ST-CENTURY ENVIRONMENTAL CHALLENGES

Sample Thesis: Nations in the 21st century must find a balance between the cost of environmental policies that address global warming and the immediate and potential benefits of such policies. Additionally, international leaders, as well as global businesses, have recognized that inaction regarding the environment may be even more costly than action, in the long run.

Sample Closing Paragraph: The Canadian Prime Minister outlined the concerns of many industrialized nations at the UN Climate Summit when he said that the "core principle" must be "balance." While most of the representatives at this 2007 meeting expressed concerns for the environment, several echoed Canada's temperance. In terms of the benefits of new environmental policies aimed at diminishing greenhouse gases, delegates included future economic positioning and survival of the planet, but the UN Secretary-General expressed an underlying fear that "the cost of inaction will far outweigh the cost of action." Nations overwhelmingly saw a need to find a balance between environmental and economic policy decisions, while remembering that inaction holds its own cost.

The Other Question Types
The New AP Multiple-Choice

Document analysis for Questions 1-2.

Document 1

SUMMARIZE – Vasari praises Brunelleschi's ingenuity and genius for rediscovering classical architecture.

ANALYZE – The document supports the contention that Brunelleschi was a major figure in Renaissance architecture.

CRITICIZE – The book's title lends credence to our analysis. Of course, if you know something about Vasari, you might suspect that his estimation of greatness may not have been universal.

Document 2

SUMMARIZE – Since this is a photograph, your summary should be a description of the picture. The image shows the rooftops of Florence and, in the center, the Duomo towers above everything. Brunelleschi's dome is and must be the centerpiece.

ANALYZE – The image highlights the importance of the dome to the Florentine skyline, and so to the city itself.

CRITICIZE – Because the photo is focused on the dome, we could say that the photographer saw the structure as the centerpiece of the city.

1. This question requires you to compare what you know about Renaissance values with what you think is portrayed in the documents. Unlike the SAQs, the correct answer is right in front of you, so you should combine your document analysis with your understanding of the given answer choices. If Generalism were the correct answer, then Brunelleschi would have been described

as a multitalented artist. Secularism emphasizes our life on earth instead of focusing on the afterlife. Skepticism questions everything. Classicism is a focus on the work of the ancient Greeks and Romans, and Vasari specifically praises Brunelleschi for rediscovering the ancient architectural forms. Additionally, the focal point of the photo is Brunelleschi's dome, and the dome is a Roman creation. B is the correct response.

2. A is the Duomo of Milan—a gothic structure. Although C and D are both Renaissance works, C utilizes a form of sculpture—the relief—which is almost a painting. D is a painting of a religious subject that had been the focus of art throughout the middle ages. Only B illustrates a form of sculpture that was common in the classical period, but fell out of style until the Renaissance—sculpture in the round.

Document analysis for Questions 3-4.

SUMMARIZE – Rousseau suggests that our true nature is shown by the sensations we choose to seek or avoid, before habit makes us change. Basically, he tells us to trust our feelings.

ANALYZE – The document supports the Romantic emphasis on emotion and feeling. Although it is not explicitly anti-reason, you might agree that Rousseau seems to be espousing heart over mind.

CRITICIZE – Rousseau was a product of the Enlightenment, but he is often called the Father of Romanticism. Can you see how Romantics might find evidence of their philosophy in Rousseau's writing?

3. C – Romanticism. The correct answer comes straight from our document analysis.

4. A – William Blake is the only choice whose work fits squarely within the Romantic school.

Document analysis for Questions 5-6.

Document

SUMMARIZE – Mrs. Smart describes her work hours and how they impact her family life. She says that she works many hours and that her family helps to care for her children.

ANALYZE – The document supports generalizations about working conditions during the industrial revolution—long hours and difficult family life.

CRITICIZE – The title indicates that Mrs. Smart was interviewed in 1843 London as part of a government report. It is reasonable to assume that Mrs. Smart was speaking truthfully because the details of her testimony are very specific and personal. It is also interesting to note that this report focused on agricultural workers, showing they were also impacted by industrialization, as were the urban laborers.

5. B – the Second Industrial Revolution

6. This is a difficult question because choices A and C seem to target the correct era, but they both specify urban factory problems. D deals with politics. B, the correct answer, addresses the role of women. During the Victorian period, women were brought in from the farm and made to be active and attentive mothers.

Document analysis for Questions 7-8.

Document

SUMMARIZE – Ellinas argues that wind power is the best solution to the urgent problem of climate change. He says that wind technology is ready and able to do the job, despite a lack of wind on Cyprus.

ANALYZE – The document appears to be the reasoned opinion of a wind power expert.

CRITICIZE – Ellinas is identified as "chairman of DK Wind Supply." It is possible that a wind executive is motivated by economic gain.

7. Once you understand that the document deals with the nexus of climate change and economics, you can eliminate B, C, and D, because they all address political issues. Only A, the Copenhagen Summit, focused on climate change and its economic impact.

8. Answer D, the correct response, is an example of a specialist with professional and economic ties to a particular solution, arguing for that solution. A and B are examples of experts sharing their expert opinions without any explicit economic benefits to themselves. Although a Volvo CEO (answer C) stands to benefit economically from improved MPG, he has no particular authority in the field of computer technology.

The Other Question Types   Short-Answer Questions

1. Analysis of the document prompt:

SUMMARIZE – Pope Nicholas offers assistance to the Byzantine emperor in return for his acceptance of the unification of the Church. It is clear from the Pope's words and his implications that his offer is entirely dependent upon the unification of the Church. No union, no help.

ANALYZE – The document helps us to better understand the gravity of the situation in Constantinople at the time, and it demonstrates the leverage of the western Roman Catholic Church. The Pope must have seen a clear advantage over Constantine to have offered such an ultimatum.

CRITICIZE – In 1452, Emperor Constantine is very much out of options regarding his defense of the empire against the ongoing assault of the Ottomans. Only under these dire circumstances could Pope Nicholas expect to coerce the emperor in this way.

(A) The events leading to this demand are many and cumulative over a great many years. You might explain the increasing threat of Ottoman attack on Constantinople, escalated by the ascension of Mehmet II to the Ottoman throne. You could also include information about the Great Schism of 1054 and the value of a successful reunification to the Pope's legacy.

(B) The immediate result of Pope Nicholas' demand was that Constantine accepted at least some of the Pope's terms and humiliated himself in the eyes of his people. Neither his diminished image nor the Pope's unfulfilled promise helped with the Byzantine defense of the city. So the long-term impact of this ultimatum was the defeat of Constantinople and the establishment of a new Ottoman capital that remains one of the most important Muslim cities even today.

(C) There are several examples of Church pressure on political figures with which you may be familiar. Henry VIII was threatened with excommunication if he divorced his wife, and the Holy Roman Emperor was pressured to turn over Martin Luther when he challenged Church teachings.

2.   Analysis of the document prompt:

SUMMARIZE – Busbecq describes the horrible effects of civil war in France. His language and tone certainly imply that he is appalled and saddened by the changes.

ANALYZE – The document adds to our understanding of the extent of the French Wars of Religion. It may be too easy to view this civil war as simply a religious dispute, but Busbecq's words remind us that it was a bloody and brutal political affair as well.

CRITICIZE – Because Busbecq is an outsider in France, his obvious horror is all the more genuine—he may have no real vested interest in the underlying dispute. Of course, his boss, the Holy Roman Emperor, may have just such an interest and Busbecq may be using language that appeals to the emperor's predispositions.

(A) Among the causes of the French Wars of Religion are the rise of the Huguenots, the struggle for control of the French throne, and the events of the Saint Bartholomew's Day Massacre.

(B) One immediate result was the War of the Three Henrys which further resulted in the ascension of the Bourbon family to the throne. Furthermore, like similar disputes in the Holy Roman Empire which ended with the Peace of Augsburg, the French Wars of Religion did not entirely end the problem of Calvinism within Catholic territories. Both failed resolutions contributed to the start of the Thirty Years War.

(C) As mentioned above, the German kingdoms experienced a very similar civil war based on religious/political disputes between Protestants and Catholics. The results were as described in part B.

3. Here the question begins with a brief statement rather than a document. You are told of a historical debate about Protestantism in England. Your response might resemble a part of an outline for an essay addressing this debate.

(A) Among the dozens of acceptable pieces of evidence is the fact that Henry VIII needed to take drastic measures to defend himself against his Catholic opponents and their followers. For instance, he executed his good friend Sir Thomas More as a show of strength, which demonstrated the lengths to which the king was willing to go to achieve his goals, and he utilized the Star Chamber to attack his political opponents. Additionally, the reign of Mary I is itself evidence of the continued power of the Catholics in England, a power which exerted itself beyond Mary's reign and threatened to topple Elizabeth I soon after her coronation.

(B) Some evidence that might help to undermine this argument is the brutality of Mary I (Bloody Mary) in her efforts to suppress a very popular Protestant faith. Additionally, the fact that Mary's young half-sister, Elizabeth, was even permitted to ascend to the throne is evidence of some significant Protestant support in England at that time.

4.   Analysis of the document prompts:

Document 1

SUMMARIZE – The document describes a time in retrospect when people had no ailments and life was orderly. He says the foreigners changed that.

ANALYZE – As an eyewitness to the changes, this speaker may have some insight into the actual conditions on the Yucatan before and after the arrival of the Spanish. The document provides a perspective that can only be seen through the eyes of an aborigine.

CRITICIZE – By the year 1550, the Spanish had controlled the Yucatan for more than 30 years. This interviewee was remembering a situation that hadn't existed for almost half of a century. It is possible, especially in light of the Spanish brutality the speaker must have witnessed more recently, that he is expressing more nostalgia than history.

Document 2

SUMMARIZE – The artist contrasts the awkwardness of a Comanche on and off of his horse, implying that the Comanche is only at home on the horse.

ANALYZE – The document provides an outsider's perspective on one aspect of the Comanche's life.

CRITICIZE – Because Catlin is an artist, you might assume that he has a keen eye for detail. The awe inherent in his words may be genuine, given that he is likely seeing the Comanche from a traveler's perspective.

(A) Probably the best economic developments to use in this question are those associated with the Columbian Exchange. Both documents include evidence of European influence on Americans—disease and horses. The advent of Mercantilist policies in Europe helped to lead to an increase in exploration and colonization in the Western Hemisphere, as well as trade practices that brought goods to the Americas in exchange for gold.

(B) In addition to economics, religion also helped to accelerate the exchange between Europe and the New World. The Roman Catholic Church, in an effort to counter the erosion of its flock resulting from the Protestant Reformation, sent missionaries to convert new adherents among the Native Americans.

5. Analysis of the document prompts:

Document 1

SUMMARIZE – Catherine says that she has no intention of invading and annexing any part of Poland. She implies that there is a rumor to that effect and she flatly denies those intentions.

ANALYZE – You are likely aware of the Partitions of Poland in the late 18th century. This document makes it clear that at least some of the leaders of the Polish-Lithuanian Commonwealth suspected the intentions of Catherine the Great and feared the rise of Stanislaw Poniatowski, who was openly supported by Catherine. Additionally, Catherine's strenuous denial of the intention to partition Poland seems here to be somewhat disingenuous. Shakespeare said it best: "The lady doth protest too much, methinks."

CRITICIZE – To continue the thought from the analysis above, in addition to her incredulous tone, the date of the document, 1764, lends credence to the accusation that Catherine actually intended exactly the opposite of her "declaration." In the decade leading up to that year, Poland-Lithuania had experienced radical economic, educational, and other social reforms inspired by Enlightenment ideas. The practical results of these reforms had been a significantly improved economy and a population boom, especially in the urban centers. Another, less positive, result was strong reaction from the wealthy Polish nobility, who, like their counterparts in France, feared the loss of their own privileged place in society. These reactionaries teamed with Russia to oppose the reform movement by supporting Poniatowski, who had no blood claim to the throne. In this context, it seems even more obvious that Catherine's words may be the exact opposite of her intentions.

Document 2

SUMMARIZE – This map shows the progression of the three Partitions of Poland in 1772, 1793, and 1795. According to the shading, by the end of this time period, Poland-Lithuania had been completely absorbed by Prussia, Austria, and Russia.

ANALYZE – The sheer extent of territory relinquished in each partition helps us to better understand the Polish opposition to the actions of its own Sejm (representative assembly) in approving each partition. It supports the argument that the leaders of the Sejm were either inept, corrupt, or both.

CRITICIZE – The map was apparently designed and produced in 2010, so we might assume it was meant for some historical work about the Polish Partitions. You might believe that a map is always completely unbiased, but keep in mind that someone was trying to support a particular storyline with this map. In the absence of evidence explaining the internal disputes described above, the map, by itself, seems to imply that the Partitions were entirely executed by Prussia, Austria, and Russia. In fact, if you failed to remember the history of the Partitions, wouldn't it be easy to imagine this as a military assault? Of course, it may simply be a visual representation of the Polish Partitions.

(A) The causes of Catherine's declaration and the partitions in general have been listed in the analysis above. Poland had experienced significant Enlightenment reforms that threatened the status of the wealthy Polish nobility, as well as the stability and security of the neighboring kingdoms, driving these two groups to collaborate in reaction. Russia and the Polish nobility subsequently supported the rise of Stanislaw Poniatowski and the end of the reform movement. When the reformers resisted, the Polish Sejm approved a partition of some Polish-Lithuanian territory in return for help from Prussia, Austria, and Russia to stifle the resistance. This partition of 1772 was followed by two more in 1793 and 1795, resulting eventually in the complete disappearance of Poland-Lithuania.

(B) The Partitions of Poland are rather unique in European history, but other examples of independent nations accepting a "deal with the devil" that results in short-term gains but long-term losses are not entirely rare. For instance, you might show similarities with events in northern Italy in the years before unification. The leaders of Piedmont-Sardinia allied with Napoleon III of France to drive Austria out of neighboring Lombardy and Venetia. Unfortunately, Napoleon's own interests in Italian territories then resulted in another hurdle in the drive toward a unified Italy.

6. Analysis of the document prompt:

SUMMARIZE – Tocqueville posits that the French Revolution began because the nobility, in their efforts to reform the French economy and society and to help the French poor, inadvertently inflamed the underclasses. He implies both noble intentions and ignorance of the potential impact of words on the poor.

ANALYZE – Tocqueville, a noted and skilled observer, offers an explanation of unintended consequences for the death and destruction of the French Revolution. Given what you probably already know about the revolution, Tocqueville's argument may seem interesting, but probably insufficient. It is likely that you learned about the role of the Jacobins and other reform-minded leaders of France, who often intentionally roused the ire of the poor to support their own goals. Additionally, since most of the early revolutionaries were constitutional monarchists, you could argue that their goals were not so noble as Tocqueville has implied. They wanted to take some power from the monarchy, but not really give any to the poor.

CRITICIZE – Several things within the source line are informative. The document is excerpted from a book written in 1856, 67 years after the start of the French Revolution. Even if you did not know that Tocqueville wasn't even born until 1805, you might question the accuracy of anyone's memory over 67 years. So, his skills as an observer are irrelevant and this is strictly a historical study. Additionally, you may want to consider the context surrounding Tocqueville's publication. He was probably writing amidst, or shortly after, the Revolutions of 1848, and during the time of Louis Napoleon Bonaparte's rise in France. The middle class, and very definitely anti-monarchist revolutionaries of 1848, bore little resemblance to those figures responsible for the start of the

French Revolution. It is possible that Tocqueville's opinion of the earlier people and events was tainted by his observations of their more recent counterparts.

(A) Evidence to support Tocqueville's thesis might include the events of the Great Fear when rumored threats of the king's army attacking in the countryside inspired poor farmers to rise up. The farmers' revolt was so sudden and dangerous that the National Constituent Assembly needed to stop its constitutional development and at least imply a promise of tax relief to quell the storm. Notably, the farmers never rejoined the revolution and returned to their former conservative values. In this case, it appears that talk of revolution and tax reform was the driving force of the uprising.

(B) To undermine Tocqueville's argument, you could use the example of the Sans Culottes, who intentionally inflamed the urban poor to pressure the nobility for their own purposes. In this case, it was neither inadvertent aristocratic talk nor unintentional inflammation of the poor that provoked the uprisings that led to a republican government.

(C) Whereas you may be hard pressed to cite examples to support Tocqueville, you will likely have very little difficulty finding examples of revolutions that were not caused by the careless words of well-meaning aristocrats. The Russian Revolution of 1917, for instance, began as a bubbling over of dissatisfaction with the status quo. The monarchy, in its attempt to brutally suppress disgruntled workers in St. Petersburg, inspired even more revolutionary sentiment and quickly lost control of the situation. Any number of the anti-imperialist revolts of the 20th century might also be used as evidence against Tocqueville's point.

7.   Analysis of the document prompts:

Document 1

SUMMARIZE – Rousseau details the reasons for his argument that women are essentially different from men, and that it is this difference that necessitates a unique education for women. He clearly believes that women are less able to reason abstractly than men.

ANALYZE – The document provides rather strong evidence of Rousseau's anti-gender equality perspective. For those who know Rousseau as an Enlightenment *philosophe*, his traditional view of women may be surprising.

CRITICIZE – This is an excerpt from *Emile*, one of Rousseau's seminal works. Although he was a product of the Enlightenment, Rousseau is often known as the Father of Romanticism. By 1762, he had begun to question rationalism and egalitarianism. The perspective expressed in this document is not surprising given Rousseau's other writings.

Document 2

SUMMARIZE – Wollstonecraft argues in direct opposition to Rousseau. In fact, she mentions Emile in the document itself. Her contention is that only independent and well-educated women can make good mothers.

ANALYZE – Wollstonecraft's writings get to the heart of the gender debate of the late 18th century. She is one of the author's who most persuasively argues for equality between men and women. By mentioning the role of mothers in creating good patriots, Wollstonecraft appeals to the revolutionary spirit for support of gender equality.

CRITICIZE – The title of her work, *A Vindication of the Rights of Women*, was meant to parallel the popular revolutionary work, *Declaration of the Rights of Man*, written in 1789 and one of the foundational works of the French Revolution. By 1792, the revolution had gained momentum and was quickly building to a climax in the National Convention. Wollstonecraft undoubtedly wanted to insure a place for women in the new republic, so the timing of this work could not have been more appropriate. Of course, she had been a staunch proponent of equal education for women throughout her life, publishing several other works supporting that argument, so the timing of this document was likely not just opportunistic.

(A) Political developments leading to the debate over equal education for women may be drawn from England and France in this era. Beginning with the reign of James I, British women were given a restricted education. King James was famously opposed to educating women for fear they become too sly. Later, during the Enlightenment and French Revolution, men and women began to support equal education as a means to allowing women to achieve their fullest potential, a potential which had previously been undervalued.

(B) A social development which led to, or at least accelerated, the debate over education equality was the revolutionary empowerment of women in French society. Although their political rights were not supported, women began to play a greater role in social movements. For instance, The Mothers' March on Versailles in 1789 was begun by women and supported by the men of French society.

8.   Analysis of the document prompt:

SUMMARIZE – In this secondary source document, Popiel explains a change in childrearing practices at the end of the 18th century. She says that mothers became the chief caretakers of their own children, in contrast to the wet nurses of the prior period.

ANALYZE – The document elucidates several points about 18th-century family life. It serves as evidence that mothers were not expected to care for their children before the late 18th century. In fact, the note about hanging swaddled babies on hooks conjures images of overworked wet nurses with perhaps dozens of infant charges. In contrast, by the end of the century, mothers more often nursed and cared for their own children. Popiel also suggests that this new practice was supported by Rousseau's philosophy.

CRITICIZE – Professor Popiel is a professional historian and this document is excerpted from a work of historical scholarship. Scholarly writings like these are not generated haphazardly like blog posts. These are usually the result of years of research into primary source documents, often in their original language and format. Additionally, scholarly writing is published only after a thorough peer review. This means that other scholars of 18th-century French history would have read this piece pre-publication and commented on the validity of Popiel's argument, as well as the accuracy of her evidence. I raise this point because, in our contemporary society, we tend to think that when two people have differing opinions, one is correct and the other is wrong and possibly lying. In the world of historical scholarship, however, historians with different theses can agree on the accuracy of the evidence and acknowledge opposing interpretations of that evidence.

(A) Rousseau's *Emile* is one piece of evidence that helps to connect the description to his own philosophy. In *Emile*, Rousseau makes very clear his contention that women should be educated in the skills of childrearing, and that their most useful place is in the home. Additionally, in his "Social Contract," Rousseau espouses that man is born free and society tends to suppress that freedom. Metaphorically, if not in actuality, the swaddling of babies can be seen as teaching them that they are not free. A child raised in the care of his mother, free of restrictive swaddling, will more likely grow up to be a free man.

(B) The Popiel document does not necessarily connect the change in childrearing practices to the philosophy of Rousseau. In fact, she specifically says that "if Rousseau's vision became reality, the mother would become the ideal nurse," but the implication is that, at least for a time, the wet nurses simply changed their way of caring for the children in their charge.

9. Analysis of the document prompt:

   SUMMARIZE – Marx suggests that the leaders of the Prussian revolution of 1848 represented the interests of the middle class and allied themselves to the Court, therefore, they lost the trust of the people from the start.

   ANALYZE – The document provides one perspective on the reasons for the failure of the Frankfurt Assembly and the Berlin Assembly in the spring of 1848. As Marx contends, the elected officials set out to write a constitution in support of the monarchy, and ultimately they gave way to the demands of King Frederick William.

CRITICIZE – Although his argument sounds logical enough and his facts are accurate, the views of Karl Marx are well known. On more occasions than this, he has blamed the course of history on the suppression of the working classes.

(A) The facts of the Berlin Assembly support Marx's contention directly. The representatives, in fact, did ally with the king and ultimately it was that alliance that brought about their demise. Frederick William IV imposed his own version of constitutional monarchy on the body, and subsequently replaced them with his own bicameral legislature. The aftermath of this assembly also can be used to support Marx's point. The young Junker, Otto von Bismarck, led the new legislature. Bismarck's conservative rise to power over the succeeding years resulted in the "betrayal" of the interests of the working class and the peasantry.

(B) Although the Frankfurt Assembly, which preceded the Berlin Assembly as a constitutional convention, ultimately failed, it was not necessarily the result of collaboration with the king. In fact, many historians blame the failure of the Frankfurt Assembly on the fact that its members seemed incapable of agreeing on any way forward.

10. Analysis of the document prompt:

SUMMARIZE – Bentham says that all mankind is ruled by pain and pleasure, and that the role of government is to provide the greatest happiness for the greatest number.

ANALYZE – The document explains the foundational principle for an important 19th-century theory of government—utilitarianism.

CRITICIZE – Since Bentham published this work in 1789, it is reasonable to assume that he was influenced by events leading up to the start of the French Revolution. You can probably see how his principle of the "greatest happiness for the greatest number" could be used to explain the decline of the monarchy and the uprisings of 1789.

(A) The French Revolution can be a source of evidence in support of Bentham's utilitarianism. The old regime was designed to benefit those in the top two estates of French Society, a group which represented only 2% of the population of France. As Bentham indicates in the document, utilitarianism is dangerous to a government that provides the greatest happiness for a small group. In this case, the danger led to a revolution. Democracy, as a concept, supports Bentham's theory as well. When a government is controlled by majority rule, then, by definition, it provides the greatest happiness for the greatest number.

(B) One problem with democratic rule is insuring the rights of the minority. When a majority of the voters benefit from an oppressive policy, like slavery, the "greatest happiness for the greatest number" tends to perpetuate that policy. The only way to overcome that sort of oppression is to pass laws that provide happiness for some portion of the minority.

11. Analysis of the document prompts:

Document 1

SUMMARIZE – The document details conditions under which boys worked at a particular factory. It suggests that the working conditions are so horrible they seem unbelievable, but that they are true.

ANALYZE – Here is explicit evidence of at least one factory that has taken advantage of its workers—specifically young boys who are forced to work more than 48 hours straight. It can be used to substantiate the underside of industrialization.

CRITICIZE – This document is excerpted from a factory inspector's report. We have no way to know if the inspector had a particular agenda for his report—for instance, to expose abuses or to cover up abuses. Because the report was presented to Parliament, however, it may be that the inspector attempted to be as detailed and accurate as possible to demonstrate his value in the eyes of the government.

Document 2

SUMMARIZE – This is a photograph of a man and a boy standing among the machines of a factory. The man is looking down at the boy, who appears to be staring at the machines in front of them. There seem to be many machines in this factory, but it is impossible to count them in this image.

ANALYZE – The document provides a firsthand, albeit momentary, look inside a factory. It also seems to support the contention that children were hired routinely because it appears as though the man is instructing the boy.

CRITICIZE – The citation on this document states only that it is a photograph from 1903. Without any other information, we have no way of knowing the photographer's intentions.

(A) The Second Industrial Revolution introduced mechanized industry to Europe. Because urban factories lacked a ready workforce, it was necessary that the factory owners hire women and children. As an added bonus, these groups of laborers tended to work for much lower wages than their male counterparts.

(B) As a result of child labor and the imposition of extremely long hours, eventually Parliament expanded regulations designed to restrict the power and independence of factory owners and provide greater union support for workers. Finally, in 1906, the Labour Party was formed.

(C) Similar conditions existed in Germany, where industrial production nearly doubled in the closing decades of the 19th century. There Bismarck supported better working conditions to insure the health and wellbeing of the German workers. Although he supported a healthier workforce, however, Bismarck did not support shorter hours. He, like the business owners in Germany, believed in the overwhelming benefit of hard work.

12. This question begins with a brief statement rather than a document. You are told of an historical debate about industrialization. Your response might resemble a part of an outline for an essay addressing this debate.

(A) Although industry owners in Britain were allowed to operate without much oversight in the early decades of the Second Industrial Revolution, their counterparts on the continent were much more restricted from the outset. In Germany, for example, Otto von Bismarck imposed strict guidelines governing the operation of factories and the treatment of workers. The differences in industrial regulation between Britain and Germany reflected their overall differences of government. A second example can be seen in Italy at the start of the 20th century. As Italy changed from an agricultural economy to one based on manufacturing and hydroelectricity, the old geographic divisions began to cause problems. Although Milan, Turin, and Genoa in the north were benefitting from industrialization, southern Italy lagged far behind. The Italian government stepped in early in the process to try to distribute the benefits of industry more evenly.

(B) An exception to this view of the spread of industrialization can be found in France. Here the pace of industrial growth was much slower than in either Germany or England. Consequently, the impact on the worker was gradual and the French government had less need to get involved early.

13. Analysis of the document prompt:

SUMMARIZE – Wilson outlines the basic principles underlying his Fourteen Points proposal. He says that the Fourteen Points are based on essential justice for all people, an end to imperial dominance, and self-determination of populations.

ANALYZE – This addendum to the Fourteen Points proposal serves to clarify and simplify the essential goals of the longer document. It provides evidence of Wilson's own interpretation of his intentions.

CRITICIZE – These are Woodrow Wilson's own words attempting to clarify his earlier points. He delivers this addendum about a month after he first explained the Fourteen Points, and three weeks after the opening of the Paris Peace Conference. If you are at all familiar with the conference and its participants, you may know that there was quite a bit of disagreement about what exactly constituted "justice" for Germany. Most of the

European allies wanted some form of retribution or revenge. It is possible that Wilson quickly understood that his "just peace," as outlined in the Fourteen Points, was unpalatable to his European counterparts and he was attempting here to simplify the message to its basic premise.

(A) The causes of Wilson's proposal and this addendum were the political maneuvering that led to the First World War. Secret alliances, imperial competition, unbridled nationalism, and a rapid escalation of militarism were the underlying causes of the war. Wilson tried to address each of these issues in his Fourteen Points proposal.

(B) One immediate result of Wilson's statement was a discussion among the participants at the Paris Peace Conference of the principle of justice and how it might be applied to Germany. Unfortunately for Wilson, although his proposal helped to begin this discussion, a majority of the participants did not view the principle in the same way as Wilson had when he designed the Fourteen Points. Furthermore, since Wilson was committed to his principles as outlined in the document, he was somewhat sidelined at the conference and was forced to return to the US at the end with a much different treaty than he had hoped. The ultimate result was that the Treaty of Versailles offered none of the "just peace" that Wilson had proposed and that might have prevented a future war.

14. Analysis of the document prompt:

SUMMARIZE – Reitan outlines Margaret Thatcher's successful campaign to restrict immigration to the UK from its Commonwealth territories. He suggests that she managed this feat by appealing to the basically racist sentiments of both Conservatives and Labour, who each supported the Nationality Act of 1981 for their own anti-immigrant reasons.

ANALYZE – The document is important evidence to support the strength of Thatcher's leadership as illustrated by her ability to identify common ground and cobble together the necessary votes to push through her own agenda. Reitan also provides some persuasive points to support his contention that the Thatcher years were driven by nationalism and racism.

CRITICIZE – Since this 2002 study sees the Thatcher years as "revolutionary," Reitan might be expected to overstate the impact of Thatcher herself and understate the influence of historical context. It seems, however, based on this brief excerpt, that this is not the case.

(A) This part of your answer might be based entirely on the document. The fact that the bill targets only Commonwealth immigrants—those immigrants coming from former British colonies—implies a connection with ethnic makeup. Whereas Irish, Scottish, and Welsh immigrants to Britain had always enjoyed free passage, and EU members continued to enjoy the same, immigrants from places like India were denied citizenship according to this new law.

(B) Despite the argument in Part A, you might also cite evidence from the 1990s that points to a series of new laws that restricted immigrants from Eastern Europe. As the Soviet Union and its partners crumbled, the flow of refugees from the eastern part of the continent to the UK increased dramatically. In response, Parliament passed a series of laws aimed at restricting that flow. Because these restrictions were aimed at other Europeans—ethnically similar to the British—you could argue that the Nationality Act of 1981 was just the first in a series of Conservative laws limiting all immigration to the UK.

(C) A very recent example would be Hungary's response to a flood of Syrian immigrants in 2015. The Hungarian government erected fences and posted soldiers along the border to prevent these new immigrants from entering. Similarly, Hungary and others who tried to stem the flow of these new refugees were accused of racist motives.

15. This question begins with a brief statement rather than a document. You are told of a historical debate about the Interwar artistic movements. Your response might resemble a part of an outline for an essay addressing this debate.

(A) One art form that is often cited as originating from revulsion to war was Dadaism. Dada artists defied traditional artistic standards to such an extent that their work was often called anti-art art. Similarly, Surrealism was another school of art that rejected the traditional forms in favor of images based on imagination and dreams. Artists like Salvador Dali typified Surrealism. These two schools sometimes self-identified as anti-war, and serve as evidence that interwar art was a reaction to the First World War.

(B) Expressionist paintings are sometimes lumped together with Surrealist and Dadaist works as reactions to the horrors of war. Expressionist artists, however, specifically denied this connection. In fact, many expressionists, like Franz Marc and Edvard Munch, produced works that predated the end of the war.

16. Analysis of the document prompt:

SUMMARIZE – Subteiny details some of the horrors of the Great Purge of 1937 in Ukraine. He lists the many Ukrainian groups that were eliminated in mass executions which may have numbered in the hundreds of thousands.

ANALYZE – The evidence presented in this document is important to our understanding of the brutality of the Soviet regime under Stalin. Additionally, it lends credence to the argument that Ukrainians were victims of one of the greatest mass murders in history.

CRITICIZE – All we know from the source line is the author, title, and date of publication. In this case, the information gives us very little on which we might base our assessments.

(A) The Great Purge was the result of Stalin's attempt to eliminate all political opposition, and, in the case of Ukraine, gain complete control over the "breadbasket of Eastern Europe." His ruthlessness led to the murder of hundreds of thousands.

(B) The impact of the purge on the Ukrainian mentality is beyond description. But one specific effect was that the Ukrainians welcomed the Nazi army when it invaded in 1941. After losing so many to the Stalinist purge, the Ukrainians saw the Nazis as saviors. Of course, thousands more died at the hands of the Nazis in the winter of 1941-42. As a further insult, the Ukrainians were labeled Nazi collaborators at the end of the war, a label that persists in some circles even today.

(C) Perhaps the simplest parallel is France during the Terror. Just like Stalin, the leaders of the Committee of Public Safety targeted thousands of political opponents for execution.

About the Author

Tony Maccarella has been teaching social studies since 1982, including over 10 years of AP European History at Parsippany Hills High School in Parsippany, New Jersey. In addition to European History, he has also taught World History, AP U.S. History, Comparative Governments, Anthropology, Psychology, Economics, and Military History.

Since 2002, Tony has served as a Reader and Table Leader for the AP European History exam. He is responsible for scoring AP European History exam questions, supervising other readers, and assisting with the clarification of scoring standards.

SHERPALEARNING
GUIDING YOU TO EVEN GREATER HEIGHTS

www.sherpalearning.com